How to Pray for
LOST
LOVED ONES

DUTCH SHEETS

Regal

A Division of Gospel Light
Ventura, California, U.S.A.

Published by Regal Books
A Division of Gospel Light
Ventura, California, U.S.A.
Printed in the U.S.A.

Regal Books is a ministry of Gospel Light, an evangelical Christian publisher dedicated to serving the local church. We believe God's vision for Gospel Light is to provide church leaders with biblical, user-friendly materials that will help them evangelize, disciple and minister to children, youth and families.

It is our prayer that this Regal book will help you discover biblical truth for your own life and help you meet the needs of others. May God richly bless you.

For a free catalog of resources from Regal Books/Gospel Light, please call your Christian supplier or contact us at 1-800-4-GOSPEL or www.regalbooks.com.

Cover and Internal Design by Robert Williams
Edited by Wil Simon and David Webb

Library of Congress Cataloging-in-Publication Data
Sheets, Dutch.
    How to pray for lost loved ones / Dutch Sheets.
      p.   cm.
    Includes bibliographical references.
    ISBN 0-8307-2765-5 (pbk.)
    1. Prayer—Christianity.   I. Title.

    BV210.2 .S5124   2001
    248.3'2—dc21   2001019706

1 2 3 4 5 6 7 8 9 10 11 12 13 14 15 / 09 08 07 06 05 04 03 02 01

Rights for publishing this book in other languages are contracted by Gospel Literature International (GLINT). GLINT also provides technical help for the adaptation, translation and publishing of Bible study resources and books in scores of languages worldwide. For further information, write to GLINT, P.O. Box 4060, Ontario, CA 91761-1003, U.S.A. You may also send e-mail to Glintint@aol.com, or visit the GLINT website at www.glint.org.

Contents

The Persistent Knocking

Author and lecturer Leo Buscaglia once talked about a contest he was asked to judge. The purpose of the contest was to find the most caring child. The winner was a four-year-old boy whose next-door neighbor was an elderly gentleman who had recently lost his wife. Upon seeing the man cry, the little boy went into the old gentleman's yard, climbed onto his lap and just sat there. When his mother asked him what he had said to the neighbor, the little boy said, "Nothing. I just helped him cry."

LETTING GOD CRY THROUGH US

On Wednesday, October 4, 2000, God somehow powerfully touched my heart with His, and for three and a half hours God allowed me to help Him cry over our nation.

Though I have often asked God for His heart toward America, I was in no way ready for the intensity with which it came that night. As I felt God's aching heart for America, I thought my own heart would break in two. I didn't know it was possible to weep from so deep within. It was not from my head or my emotions; it was from deep in my heart.

That day the Lord placed upon me an incredible burden to call the nation to prayer for the then-upcoming presidential election. I was led by the Lord to issue a prayer alert that ultimately went to millions of people, resulting in a great mobilization of prayer asking God for His man to be placed in office.

I believe God answered the prayers of those many people and gave us the president He wanted America to have. I believe He gave us a man who, like King David, is a man after His heart—a sincere, humble man who loves God and through whom He can work. Not that God is a Republican or a Democrat. It's not about a political party but about finding a person God can use to accomplish His purposes. In ancient Israel, He could not do what He wanted through King Saul, so He looked for a man after His own heart. That person, of course, was David. I believe that, in this election, God heard our prayers and graciously gave us a man after His heart to lead our nation.

My wife and I, along with a few others from our church in Colorado Springs, attended the inauguration of George W. Bush. It was worth every minute of standing in the extremely cold rain—as well as the many hours of prayer and fasting leading up to this day—as I watched and heard Bush, with great conviction, complete his oath of office by saying, "So help me God." Upon the uttering of those words, one well-known minister in attendance was heard to say, "The curse is broken off of America." I, too, believe that it marked a new beginning. We are, indeed, seeing God's grace upon us to heal and save our nation.

Another important result of my experience on October 4 was a fresh awareness of the incredible passion of the Lord to save. I already knew God desired to save America. He had been challenging me for the past few years to believe Him for the saving of this nation, for genuine revival and a great harvest of souls. But on this particular evening, it was different. I literally *felt* God's breaking heart aching to save and heal America.

In my prayers for our nation, the Lord has often led me to Ezekiel 37. In this passage He uses a graveyard of dry bones to reveal Israel's spiritually dead condition to the prophet Ezekiel. As the prophet gazed upon these dry bones, the Lord asked him an interesting question: "Can these bones live?" Ezekiel, not knowing how to respond, simply said, "Oh, Lord God, You know" (see Ezek. 37:3). God's response was to have Ezekiel prophesy to the bones and later to have the wind of the Holy Spirit breathe life into the bones. In the vision the bones came together, and the wind—or breath—of God's Spirit came to them, causing them to live again.

As I said, God has often led me to this passage. It seems I am prompted with the same question about America that God asked Ezekiel about Israel: Can these bones live? I have always tried to summon faith and believe that America will indeed receive a revival that results in Resurrection life. But I must admit there have been times of wavering in which I found it difficult to believe.

However, on that aforementioned evening something changed. I actually *felt* God's passion to save our nation. I identified with His aching heart so strongly that my faith was lifted to a new level. I knew beyond any doubt that the dry bones of America *could* live, because *God desperately wants to save this nation.*

I am fully persuaded that hundreds of thousands of people will be saved in America over the next several years. As God comes to bring salvation to our nation, however, that salvation will come *an individual at a time.* Those born again will be our fathers, mothers, sons, daughters, husbands, wives, friends and neighbors. They will have names and faces, known personally by God.

I want you to be so convinced that God will save the person you love that you would be shocked if they *didn't* get saved!

My purpose for this chapter is to encourage your faith that *God really does want to save those dear to you.* I want your faith to be lifted to a new level. I have found that where faith for the salvation of the lost is concerned, unbelief controls much of the Church. We ask God to send revival and save people, but deep in our hearts we can't believe it is really going to happen. Perhaps it's because we've prayed and waited so long that we are no longer convinced God really will do it.

PERSEVERING IN PRAYER

Chrissy sleepily answered the phone late one night and heard her older brother's voice on the line. "Sis,

I just invited Jesus into my life!" he shouted. "I'm saved! The preacher said to tell someone immediately, so I knew I had to call you because you've prayed for me for so long."

The praying sister sat speechless with the phone in her hand. This brother of hers—the one who had mocked and screamed at her at their mother's funeral when she tried to share Jesus with him—the one who had broken up a pastor's home to marry his third and current wife—this rebel was calling to say he'd accepted Jesus. She could hardly believe it!

Why is it when our loved ones are saved in answer to prayers we've prayed for years, we are always surprised? Could it be that we secretly doubt whether our prayers will really change anything? Or that we've written off the person as hopeless?[1]

I want you to be so convinced that God will save the person you love, the one for whom you pray, that you would be shocked if they *didn't* get saved. I want you to believe God is so passionately in love with people that when you cry for those you love, you realize you're really helping *Him* cry.

1st

Why is this kind of faith so important? First, if we don't really believe God will answer our prayers, we will not pray with any kind of consistency and diligence. We may sporadically ask Him, but we certainly will not persevere. We must have a motivational faith that truly believes He is hearing us and He will answer.

When Raymond's brother was dying, he stood by the hospital bed and said boldly, "Henry, I've prayed for you for years. I'm tired of you cursing the Lord I serve. It's time you accepted Him and all He has done for you! You could very well die tonight! Where would you spend eternity?"

Henry acknowledged his need for God and asked Jesus into his heart right then. Finally, after 15 years, Raymond saw his prayers for his brother dramatically answered just a few days before Henry died. [2]

Like Raymond, we must have faith that doesn't quit!

FAITH RELEASES GOD'S POWER

The second reason this issue is so important is that our faith really does release God's power. There is a striking story in Mark 6:1-6 about Christ not working any miracles in His hometown of Nazareth. A careful reading and study of the verses in the original Greek text reveals that Jesus didn't simply choose not to work miracles, but He actually could not work miracles in Nazareth because of the unbelief of the people.

I certainly am not implying that Christ did not have enough power or that something was wrong with His spiritual condition. It is clear, however, that somehow his neighbors' unbelief blocked God's power from flowing from Christ to them. The Scriptures don't say He didn't want to work miracles or that He chose not to work miracles. Mark 6:5 says, "He could do no miracle there except that He laid His hands upon a few sick people and healed them" (emphasis added).

There really is a dynamic of faith wherein unbelief can hinder God's power from flowing to us. In James 1:6,7, we are instructed:

I lack faith.

Ask in faith without any doubting, for the one who doubts is like the surf of the sea driven and tossed by the wind. For let not that man expect that he will receive anything from the Lord.

Again, from this passage it is clear that unbelief can cause us to not receive what we have asked for, even though it may be within the scope of God's will.

Galatians 6:9 (*KJV*) states: "And let us not be weary in well doing: for in due season we shall reap, if we faint not." Again, if we are not able to persevere, which certainly has to do with our faith, then there will be times when we will not reap what we have asked. Jesus said, "If thou canst believe, all things are possible to him that believeth" (Mark 9:23, *KJV*, emphasis added).

It is imperative that we ask in faith when we pray for the salvation of the people we love. We must be convinced that God will answer our prayers, or we will not be sufficiently motivated to ask or to do so with persevering faith. And it is also true that unbelief will block the power of God from being released to answer the prayer.

I can well imagine that some of you are already feeling intimidated, questioning whether you have, or could ever have, enough faith to pray your loved one or friend into the family of God. The answer to your question is an emphatic yes!

Don't allow Satan, that accuser of the brethren, to defeat you before you ever get started. You are of the family of faith. The Holy Spirit, the author of faith, is in you, and you can and will be able to believe. Deep within your spirit it is your nature to walk in faith.

GOD TURNS OUR WEAKNESS INTO STRENGTH

One of my favorite stories in the Bible is that of Abraham and Sarah believing God's promise for a son. What most people don't realize, however, is that they didn't always walk in great faith during the 25 years they waited for Isaac. They wavered in their faith for receiving a son through Sarah—so much so that they conceived a plan to try to fulfill the promise through Hagar, Sarah's maid. Ishmael was the result.

The aged couple were still in doubt when God came again and said to Abraham that Sarah would conceive and bear him a son "at this season next year" (Gen. 17:21). Abraham was 99 years old and Sarah was 90. Abraham laughed at God, and so did Sarah. I probably would have laughed, too. Abraham's "faith-filled" response was, "Oh that Ishmael might live before Thee!" (Gen. 17:18). I have asked God to accept a few of my Ishmaels, too!

Interestingly, in a seeming contradiction, the New Testament states very clearly that it was because of Abraham and Sarah's *great faith* that God was able to fulfill the promise (see Rom. 4:17-22; Heb. 11:11,12). Does the New Testament contradict the Old Testament? Absolutely not.

Romans 4:20 tells us they *"grew* strong in faith" (emphasis added). And here's the good news: They grew into this incredibly strong faith in three short months, at which time Isaac was conceived. Twenty-four years of unbelief was overcome in just three months! From the point of unbelief until Isaac's conception three months later, something transpired to transform them from unbelief to the great faith spoken of in the New Testament.

If God could do this for them, He can do it for you! Abraham and Sarah were not even born again as you are. They didn't have the Holy Spirit abiding within them. Surely we who live on this side of the Cross, with a "better covenant" and "better promises" (Heb. 8:6), can rise to a level of faith as quickly, or even more so. Don't underestimate the Christ in you (see Col. 1:27)!

Sam and Jed refused to walk in anything but faith. Hearing that a $5,000 bounty had been offered for the capture or killing of wolves, they became bounty hunters. Waking up one night, Sam saw that they were surrounded by 50 pairs of gleaming eyes—ravenous wolves licking hungry chops. "Jed, wake up," he whispered to his sleeping partner. "We're rich!"

When the wolves of unbelief and opposition endeavor to erode your faith, and when the circumstances around you scream that you will never receive the Lord's promise, follow the admonition of the prophet Joel:

Let the weak say, I am strong (Joel 3:10, *KJV*).

And see the unbelievers around you not as threats but as opportunities. They really can live, and you can really believe it.

QUESTIONS FOR WISDOM AND FAITH

doubt

1. Why do we fail to be persistent in our prayers?
2. Can a person pray in faith for someone's salvation and not seemingly see this prayer fulfilled? If so, why would this happen? *Because God's timing is not ours. Love must remain faithful.*
3. Why does God allow us to experience a small measure of His long-suffering heart over the salvation of other people? *So we can see + feel the depth of His love for the unsaved!*

15

Faith Paves the Way

There is an old story that recalls how Satan once summoned his top demonic aides to plan strategy against the Church of Jesus Christ. Satan stood at the blackboard lecturing and illustrating the latest tactics in demonic warfare. At the end of this session Satan said, "Now get out there and give your best possible effort to keep believers from winning the lost!" As the demonic hierarchy headed for the door, Satan hollered out, "By the way, be careful! If those Christians ever begin to really believe and act on what they have in the Word of God, then hell help us, all heaven's going to break loose!"

Well, we ARE going to believe. And we ARE going to break heaven loose over people!

GOD'S ASSURANCE

As stated in the first chapter, faith is necessary in order for us to receive our provisions in Christ. The generation of Israel that came out of bondage in Egypt did not receive their inheritance because of their inability to believe. Hebrews 4:1,2 tells us:

> Therefore, let us fear lest, while a promise remains of entering His rest, any one of you should seem to have come short of it. For indeed we have had good news preached to us, just as they also; but the word they heard did not profit them, because it was not united by faith in those who heard.

In this chapter we are going to see how our faith can grow to a point where we become assured of seeing God's salvation come to those for whom we pray. First, here are some principles of faith that are essential for us to understand.

Though it may seem obvious, I need to state that faith is not of the mind—it is not positive thinking. It is possible to convince ourselves of something mentally and allow no thoughts of doubt to enter our minds without that being true biblical faith. Biblical faith is of the heart, not the mind (see Mark 11:23; Rom. 10:10).

Hebrews 11:1 says faith is an assurance of what we ask for—things hoped for. The word "assurance" comes from

---

If you do not have a deep, settled faith that you will see the salvation of the one for whom you are praying, don't be intimidated. Your faith simply needs to grow.

---

the Greek word *hupostasis*.[1] This was also the Greek word for a title deed. Biblical faith is knowing with certainty deep in our hearts that we have what we ask God for, just as surely as a title deed proves that we own a piece of property.

The same verse in the *King James Version* tells us that faith is our evidence of things we cannot see. "Evidence" is from the Greek word *elegchos*,[2] which literally means the proof of the charges in a legal court case that results in a conviction. The word was used in a court of law for evidence significant enough to prove a case and result in a conviction. In other words, our faith in God's Word or His promises is all the evidence we need to validate our conviction.

If there is not a deep, settled faith in you for the salvation of the one for whom you are praying—or for anything else for that matter—please don't be intimidated. Your faith simply needs to grow. The Bible teaches that faith is like a mustard seed. The point of Jesus' mustard seed parable is not that we need faith the size of a mustard seed. Though some translations word it that way, it is not entirely accurate. Jesus does not tell us we need faith *the size of* a mustard seed. He says we need faith that is *like* a mustard seed. The point is that the seed starts out tiny but grows into a tree.

Romans 12:3 teaches that each of us is given "a measure of faith." The Greek word *metron*, which is translated "measure," means "a limited portion."[3] Romans 1:17, however, states that we go from faith to faith. In other words, our faith must grow.

Paul commended the Thessalonian church, saying, "Your faith is greatly enlarged" (2 Thess. 1:3). *Huperauxano*, the Greek word translated "greatly enlarged," means "to increase above ordinary degree."[4] Our faith can do this also.

Earlier I referred to Romans 4, where it says that Abraham grew strong in faith. The phrase being "fully assured" in

Romans 4:21 is very significant. It comes from the Greek word *plerophoreo*, which is a combination of the words *pleros*, meaning "full," and *phero*, meaning "to carry."[5] Together they give us the literal definition "to bring in full measure." In other words, Abraham started with a measure of faith that grew to full measure.

How does this happen?

NURTURING THE SEEDS OF FAITH

Our faith grows by a revelation of the Word of God as we feed and meditate on it (see Josh. 1:8; Ps. 1:2; Rom. 10:17). Doing this transforms God's Word from a seed (see Mark 4:1-9,13-20; 1 Pet. 1:23) to full fruition.

We start with a promise from God's Word. As we meditate on that promise, the Holy Spirit infuses it with His life, causing it to grow and multiply in us. Our part is to feed on and meditate in the Word of God. The Holy Spirit's part is to cause it to grow.

George Müller, a great man of faith, had this to say about the maturing of our faith:

You ask how may I, a true believer, have my faith strengthened? Here is the answer: "Every good gift and every perfect gift is from above, and comes down from the Father of lights, with whom there is no variation or shadow of turning" (Jas. 1:17, *NKJV*). As the increase of faith is a good gift, it must come from God; therefore, He ought to be asked for this blessing. The following means, however, ought to be used.

First, carefully read the Word of God and meditate on it. Through reading the Word of God, and especially through meditation on the Word of God, the believer becomes more acquainted with the nature and character of God. Thus he sees more and more, besides His holiness and justice, what a kind, loving, gracious, merciful, mighty, wise and faithful God He is.

He will rely upon the willingness of God to help him because he has not only learned from the Scriptures what a kind, good, merciful, gracious and faithful being God is; but he has also seen in the Word of God how, in a great variety of instances, God has proved Himself to be so. And the consideration of this, if God has become known to us through prayer and meditation on His own Word, will lead us with a measure of confidence, in general at least, to rely upon Him. Thus the reading of the Word of God, together with meditation on it, will be one special means to strengthen our faith.[6]

As we approach God's Word with the intention of planting seeds that can grow into great faith, we should meditate specifically on scriptures that pertain to our need. In other words, if you need faith for someone's salvation, feed on promises relating to that subject. If you need to increase your faith in God as your provider, meditate on Scriptures that address this particular area of truth.

Perhaps a short explanation of biblical meditation is appropriate. Scriptural meditation does not mean attempting to clear the mind, as in Transcendental Meditation. I am not talking about having a blank mind in order to receive any and every thought communication that might be sent our way. This unbiblical form of meditation gives way to demonic thoughts.

Biblical meditation, however, means to ponder, muse on, think about and even mutter to one's self. In other words, it is repetitious thinking on and speaking of God's Word. This allows the Holy Spirit to transform the Word from information in the mind to revelation of the heart.

TEN SIGNPOSTS TOWARD GOD'S SAVING GRACE

I would like to give you 10 proofs from the Scriptures that God wants to save your loved ones. As you think and meditate on these truths, they will cause your faith to grow and you, too, will have great faith—a full measure! The Holy Spirit may give you other Scriptures, too. In no way do I consider this list to be complete.

God Wants All to Be Saved
The Scriptures tell us that God is "not willing that any should perish, but that all should come to repentance"

23

(2 Pet. 3:9, *KJV*). He could not make His will any clearer. It is His desire for every person to believe upon Christ and be born again. We don't have to wonder what God wants for the person for whom we are praying.

God Is Able to Save

②

"Behold, the LORD'S hand is not so short that it cannot save" (Isa. 59:1). We must believe not only that God wants to but that He *can* save. He is not weak; He *can* do this. His hand is very powerful and somehow He can bend, shape and change the perspective of unbelievers and bring them to a realization and understanding of the truth. He can break off of them every satanic stronghold and bring them to a knowledge of the truth.

While hitchhiking home, Roger Simms was picked up by an older gentleman in an expensive car. They talked about many things, including Mr. Hanover's business in Chicago. Roger felt a strong compulsion to witness, but was apprehensive about witnessing to a wealthy businessman. Finally, nearing his destination, Roger spoke up.

"Mr. Hanover," began Roger, "I want to share something very important with you." He explained the way of salvation and asked if Mr. Hanover would like to receive Christ as his Savior. To Roger's astonishment, the businessman pulled over to the side of the road, bowed his head, wept and prayed the prayer of salvation. He thanked Roger, saying,

"This is the greatest thing that has ever happened to me."

Five years later, while in Chicago on a business trip, Roger went to Hanover Enterprises. The receptionist told him it would be impossible to see Mr. Hanover, but Mrs. Hanover was available. A little disappointed, he followed her into an office.

After exchanging greetings, Roger explained how Mr. Hanover had kindly given him a ride years ago. Suddenly interested, Mrs. Hanover asked when this had happened. When Roger told her it was on May 7, five years earlier, she asked if anything unusual had happened during his ride.

Roger hesitated, wondering if giving his witness had been a source of contention. But, feeling the prompting of the Lord, he told her that he had shared the gospel message and that her husband had accepted the Lord into his heart.

She began to sob uncontrollably. After a few minutes, she explained that she had thought her prayers for her husband's salvation had not been answered. After leaving Roger at his destination, Mr. Hanover had died that day in a horrible head-on collision.[7]

God is faithful, and He is definitely capable!

Salvation Is His to Give

"Salvation belongs to the LORD" (Ps. 3:8). God is a God of salvation; He owns it. Since it belongs to Him, He can give it away! It is His nature, a part of who He is, to confer His gift of salvation to people. He will do this for the person for whom you pray.

His Very Name Is Savior

"And you shall call His name Jesus, for it is He who will save His people from their sins" (Matt. 1:21). The Hebrew name *Yeshua* comes from the word *yasha*, which means "save."[8] He is called *Yeshua* because He is the Savior. Think about it: He chose to call Himself "the One who saves." He loves to save. He wants to save! Salvation is who He is. He will save your loved one, your friend, your neighbor! He wants to— it's His name.

The angel said to the shepherds, "Do not be afraid; for behold, I bring you good news of a *great joy which shall be for all the people*; for today in the city of David there has been born for you a Savior, who is Christ the Lord" (Luke 2:10,11, emphasis added).

"For it is for this we labor and strive, because we have fixed our hope on the living God, *who is the Savior of all men*, especially of believers" (1 Tim. 4:10, emphasis added).

Charles Finney shared the following testimony of a father who realized the Lord's intense desire to save his family:

I knew a father who was a good man, but who had misconceptions about the prayer of faith. His whole family of children had grown up, without one of them being converted. One day his son grew ill and seemed ready to die. The father prayed, but the son grew worse and was sinking into the grave without hope. The father prayed until his anguish was unutterable. He finally prayed (there seemed no prospect of his son surviving), pouring out his soul as if he would not be denied.

Later, he got an assurance that his son would not only live, but be converted. God also assured him that not only this one, but his whole family would be converted to God. He came into the house and told his family his son would not die. They were astonished at him. "I tell you," he said, "he will not die. And no child of mine will ever die in his sins." That man's children were all converted years ago.

What do you think of that? Was that fanaticism? If you believe it was, it is because you know nothing about the prayer of faith. Do you pray like this man prayed? Do you live in such a manner that you can offer such prayers for your children?[9]

You can. Believe in the Savior! What He did for this father, He will do for you.

God's Passion to Save

While on earth as a human, the Lord would rather reach out to save a sinner than eat (see John 4). Christ, even as a flesh-and-blood human being with very real human appetites, cared much more about saving an immoral, hurting, lonely woman than about meeting His own needs.

He found much more excitement and satisfaction in saving the lost than in feeding His body. Immediately afterward, when encouraged by His disciples to eat, He simply said, "I have food to eat that you do not know about" (John 4:32). He was so excited about what happened with this lady that He had lost His appetite!

He Was Willing to Become Human to Save Us

While in heaven as God, He chose to become human in order to save us rather than to remain God only. In other words, He went to the unfathomable extent of becoming a human in order to save humanity. It meant that much to Him. He loves us so much that He would rather pay the price of becoming one of us than for us to remain outside His family. "For there is one God, and one mediator also between God and men, the man Christ Jesus" (1 Tim. 2:5).

He Was Willing to Die to Save Us

When faced with the agony of the cross, which was for our salvation, Jesus chose torture, humiliation and death instead of angelic deliverance. He could have called upon legions of angels to deliver Him (see Matt. 26:53). His desire to save us was and is so intense that no price or sacrifice was too great. He did it for your loved one. Go ahead, put a face to the price He paid!

In his book *Written in Blood*, Robert Coleman tells the story of a little boy whose sister needed a blood transfusion. The doctor had explained that she had the same disease the boy had recovered from two years earlier. Her only chance for recovery was a transfusion from someone who had previously conquered the disease. Since the two children had the same rare blood type, the boy was the ideal donor.

"Would you give your blood to Mary?" the doctor asked.

Johnny hesitated. His lower lip started to tremble. Then he smiled and said, "Sure, for my sister."

Soon the two children were wheeled into the hospital room—Mary, pale and thin; Johnny, robust and healthy. Neither spoke, but when their eyes met, Johnny grinned.

As the nurse inserted the needle into his arm, Johnny's smile faded. He watched the blood flow through the tube. With the ordeal almost over, his voice, slightly shaky, broke the silence, "Doctor, when do I die?"

Only then did the doctor realize why Johnny had hesitated, why his lip had trembled when he'd agreed to donate his blood. He'd thought giving his blood to his sister meant giving up his life. In that brief moment, he'd made his great decision.

Johnny, fortunately, didn't have to die to save his sister. Each of us, however, has a condition more serious than Mary's, and it required Jesus to give not just His blood but His life.[10]

He did it gladly.

God Desires to Show Mercy

God was willing to spare an entire wicked city, Sodom, even though it was so profoundly wicked. He told Abraham He would spare the city if even 10 righteous people could be found (see Gen. 18:32). He desires to show mercy rather than judgment toward sinners. If He was willing to spare Sodom, He is willing to spare your friend or family member—yes, even if they are bound by great perversion.

Jesus Came to Seek and Save the Lost

Jesus said He came to seek—what a great word—and to save the lost (see Luke 19:10). He is still seeking them today. He is on a quest. Let Him use you to satisfy His seeking heart! Speak this truth to your heart every day. Go to sleep at night thinking about it. Faith will come.

Salvation Is the Theme of the Bible

The Bible is the story of God's desire to save a fallen human race. The book of Genesis brings us very quickly to the Fall. The rest of the Bible is God's story of His heart toward the human race and His plan to save us from our sins.

After much worry and stress, author Quin Sherrer came to a point of faith for her three children to be touched by God's transforming power. Let her testimony encourage you as you allow your faith to grow:

Though the Scriptures boldly declare God's almighty power and Christ's victory over Satan, we often struggle to believe that His Word is really true *for us*.

Or that His power and victory will be applied to our situation.

Paul Billheimer states, "Unbelief in the integrity of the Word is the first great cause for prayerlessness." We must put our confidence in the reliability of God's Word and choose to believe God is who He says He is, and that He will do what He said He will do.

When I began diligently praying for my children, the Lord led me to meditate on this verse: "All your children shall be taught by the LORD, and great shall be the peace of your children" (Isa. 54:13, *NKJV*).

Some weeks later, after putting one child on a plane following a Labor Day visit, my heart was heavy. There was no indication of a turning toward the Lord. In church later that day, as I closed my eyes in prayer, I suddenly had an inner vision of all three of our children with arms raised, praising the Lord.

I went home and recorded it in my prayer diary. I began to declare with my mouth, "The Lord *is* my children's teacher . . . their peace shall be great. Thank you, Lord, that You will fulfill Your promise, and someday I *will* see them praising You."

Eight months later, each child came from a different city to meet me in Orlando for Mother's Day. During worship in church that morning, I looked up to see all three of them, hands raised, praising the Lord! What a Mother's Day gift!

I learned what I say with my mouth is important. It is all too easy to talk about the negatives in a situation, when instead I should open my mouth to wield the Sword of the Spirit by quoting the Word of God and declaring what God says in the matter (see Heb. 4:12).[11]

God's heart is to save. Meditate on and feed your heart with these truths, as well as any He may reveal to you. You will soon become fully convinced that the God who saves, will. Then, according to Psalm 126:5,6, after you help Him cry, you can help Him rejoice!

Bedrock for Your Faith

Here are several additional Scriptures you can meditate on to build your faith:

Crying Out to God
The LORD hears when I call to Him (Ps. 4:3).

I have called upon Thee, for Thou wilt answer me, O God (Ps. 17:6).

But as for me, I will watch expectantly for the LORD; I will wait for the God of my salvation. My God will hear me (Mic. 7:7).

And it will come about that whoever calls on the name of the LORD will be delivered (Joel 2:32).

Hunger for His Blessing

Wilt Thou not Thyself revive us again, that Thy people may rejoice in Thee? Show us Thy lovingkindness, O LORD, and grant us Thy salvation (Ps. 85:6,7).

For I will pour out water on the thirsty land and streams on the dry ground; I will pour out My Spirit on your offspring, and My blessing on your descendants (Isa. 44:3).

Wooing People to His Kingdom

He that winneth souls is wise (Prov. 11:30, *KJV*).

Now all these things are from God, who reconciled us to Himself through Christ, and gave us the ministry of reconciliation, namely, that God was in Christ reconciling the world to Himself, not counting their trespasses against them, and He has committed to us the word of reconciliation (2 Cor. 5:18,19).

Praying in Faith

If you abide in Me, and My words abide in you, ask whatever you wish, and it shall be done for you (John 15:7).

Truly, truly, I say to you, if you shall ask the Father for anything, He will give it to you in My name. Until now you have asked for nothing in My name; ask, and you will receive, that your joy may be made full (John 16:23,24).

Believe in the Lord Jesus, and you shall be saved, you and your household (Acts 16:31).

The effective prayer of a righteous man can accomplish much (James 5:16).

God's Touch of Salvation

The LORD has bared His holy arm in the sight of all the nations, that all the ends of the earth may see the salvation of our God (Isa. 52:10).

Thus says the LORD, "Preserve justice, and do righteousness, for My salvation is about to come and My righteousness to be revealed" (Isa. 56:1).

And all flesh shall see the salvation of God (Luke 3:6).

For the grace of God has appeared, bringing salvation to all men (Titus 2:11,12).

Hence, also, He is able to save forever those who draw near to God through Him, since He always lives to make intercession for them (Heb. 7:25).

God's Amazing Love

"For I have no pleasure in the death of anyone who dies," declares the LORD God. "Therefore, repent and live" (Ezek. 18:32).

For the Son of Man has come to save that which was lost (Matt. 18:11).

Thus it is not the will of your Father who is in heaven that one of these little ones perish (Matt. 18:14).

I tell you that in the same way, there will be more joy in heaven over one sinner who repents, than over ninety-nine righteous persons who need no repentance (Luke 15:7).

For God so loved the world, that He gave His only begotten Son, that whoever believes in Him should not perish, but have eternal life (John 3:16).

But we should always give thanks to God for you, brethren beloved by the Lord, because God has chosen you from the beginning for salvation through sanctification by the Spirit and faith in the truth (2 Thess. 2:13,14).

It is a trustworthy statement, deserving full acceptance, that Christ Jesus came into the world to save sinners (1 Tim. 1:15).

QUESTIONS FOR WISDOM AND FAITH

1. How do you express your faith on a daily basis?
2. When is your faith the weakest? When is it the strongest?
3. Is there a difference between faith that is nurtured over time and the gift of faith the apostle Paul describes in 1 Corinthians 12:9?
4. What is the most powerful or inspiring passage of Scripture that builds your faith? Why?

Being Strategic in Salvation

An executive hirer, a "head-hunter" who goes out and hires corporate executives for other firms, once told Josh McDowell, "When I get an executive that I'm trying to hire for someone else, I like to disarm him. I offer him a drink, take my coat off, then my vest, undo my tie, throw up my feet and talk about baseball, football, family, whatever, until he's all relaxed. Then, when I think I've got him relaxed, I lean over, look him square in the eye and say, 'What's your purpose in life?' It's amazing how top executives fall apart at that question.

"Well, I was interviewing this fellow the other day, had him all disarmed, with my feet up on his desk, talking about football. Then I leaned up and said, 'What's your purpose in life, Bob?' And he said, without blinking an eye, 'To go to heaven and take as many people with me as I can.' For the first time in my career I was speechless."[1]

As Christians, that's our purpose, too. And we're going to fulfill it.

REMOVING THE VEIL

Acts 13:36 says that King David "served the purpose of God in his own generation." Our purpose as a generation is to bring in the greatest harvest of souls the world has ever seen. What an honor! But to accomplish that purpose, we have some important and fulfilling work to do. And much of it involves strategic prayer to loose our loved ones from Satan's grasp.

The Bible tells us there is a veil that keeps unbelievers from clearly seeing the gospel:

> And even if our gospel is veiled, it is veiled to those who are perishing, in whose case the god of this world has blinded the minds of the unbelieving, that they might not see the light of the gospel of the glory of Christ, who is the image of God (2 Cor. 4:3,4).

The word "veiled" is translated from the Greek word *kalupsis*, which means "to hide, cover up, wrap around."[2] It is important to realize that unbelievers don't see the gospel because they *can't* see it. There is a veil, or covering, over their minds that prevents them from clearly seeing the light and truth of the gospel. We have been given a part to play in lifting this veil off their minds.

Related to this concept of the veil is the Greek word for "revelation," *apokalusis*. This word is simply the prefix *apo*, which means "off or away,"[3] added to the word *kalupsis*. Literally, then, a revelation is an unveiling, or uncovering. Until unbelievers have an unveiling—a revelation—they won't, indeed they can't, understand the gospel because the veil prevents them from comprehending it. Satan's goal is to hide the truth of the gospel in order to keep unbelievers in his grasp.

Before Tom was saved, he had this to say about his inability to comprehend the gospel: "As clear and simple as the gospel is to me now, it was just as confusing to me before. Oh, I thought I understood it, but I now know it was going right over my head. Then one day it was as though someone peeled back a covering and, for the first time, I truly understood what was being said."

What gives place to this veil? How does Satan, as 2 Corinthians 4:4 says, blind the minds of the unbelieving? The word "blinded" in this verse comes from the Greek word *tuphloo*, which means "to dull the intellect; to make blind."[4] Satan has an ability to dull the unbeliever's thinking where the gospel is concerned. The root word of *tuphloo*, *tupho*, has the meaning of making smoke.[5] Therefore, the blindness in this passage can be compared to a smoke screen that clouds or darkens the air to the point that a person cannot see clearly.

From this same root comes the word *tuphoo* that is used for being high-minded, proud or inflated with self-conceit.[6] The picture is of one who is "puffed up," much like smoke puffs up or billows. The blindness of the unbeliever to the gospel is directly linked to the root of pride that Satan passed on to humankind in the Garden.

The root of pride that came at the Fall causes unbelievers to think humanity's knowledge is greater than God's. This leads not to a knowledge dependent on God but to an independent knowledge that looks to one's own mind and intellect as the judge of truth. This inward quest for knowledge glorifies one's own reasoning ability and causes a rejection of God's knowledge. Because everything is filtered through this inward knowledge, all of which is inundated with pride, it usually translates into the exalting and serving of self and its desires.

Simply stated, *self* loves *self* and anything that satisfies and exalts *self*. Any message that preaches *self-denial*, or even that *self* needs to be saved (which certainly includes the gospel), is offensive to *self*.

The only answer to this self-god is death—the Cross—where we die with Christ. The only problem is self wants so desperately to live. The very nature of pride is to be self-serving and preserving. Thus, the very thing that needs to die is bent on living and must remain the enemy of God in order to do so. No wonder Paul said, "O wretched man that I am!" (Rom. 7:24, *KJV*).

Dealing Pride a Death Blow

Understanding this blinding ability of pride provides a tremendous clue in how to pray effectively for the lost. We must attack the root of pride! Most rejection of Christ, whether from the works motivation of most false religions or the simple fact that most people don't want to give lordship of their lives to another, is due to the veil of pride. This satanically initiated stronghold is the ultimate enemy of Christ and will be dealt with in finality when every knee bows and every tongue confesses that Christ is Lord. Pride will be dealt its final blow!

Ern Grover tells the following story of visiting a woman who had recently become blind:

Mrs. Avery, a woman who had recently lost her sight, invited me to join her outside in the dusk for a cup of tea. On the way outside, she scooped up a handful of cat food. She capably navigated her way to her usual seat at the table in her tiny yard. I sat down beside her and in complete darkness we listened to the sounds of her world. She identified crickets, bullfrogs, a passing motorist, the neighbor's barking dog and the meow of Mrs. Blackwell's cat. She asked me to take her hand and to point it at the north star. I started to get misty-eyed, witnessing this woman, a friend to many, coping with her new challenge of blindness. We sat sipping our tea in silent companionship for a few minutes.

Reaching into her pocket, she fingered a few of the dry nuggets of cat food. Making a "kissing" noise, she held her hand close to the ground. I could barely see the image of a cat sauntering toward her chair and nuzzling its nose in the palm of her hand. A second and then a third cat emerged from the darkness. As I watched her feed and pet her little friends, I smiled at her kindness.

As my eyes adjusted to the dark and my vision became clearer, I almost leaped out of my chair when I realized she was feeding a family of skunks!

Holding my seat, gritting my teeth and hoping I wouldn't startle her little friends, I nervously took another sip of tea. Her conversation never wavered as she continued to feed and pat the skunks circling her ankles. Then, as quickly and stealthily as they had emerged from the dark shadows, they left.[7]

Though not caused by pride, Mrs. Avery's blindness is nonetheless a fitting picture of the reality-distorting ability of pride. Though convincing ourselves of the rightness of our self-serving lifestyles and desires, it is really a terribly odorous fallen creature we humans feed when we serve the exalted god of self.

How do we deal with the vision-altering force of pride inflicted upon us by the deceived, yet deceptive, serpent himself, Satan? The Bible offers a fascinating and enlightening passage that identifies a solution for the pride problem, as well as giving other key strategies, which we will look at in the next chapter, for effectively praying for unbelievers.

> For though we walk in the flesh, we do not war according to the flesh, for the weapons of our warfare are not of the flesh, but divinely powerful for the destruction of fortresses. We are destroying speculations and every lofty thing raised up against the knowledge of God, and we are taking every thought captive to the obedience of Christ (2 Cor. 10:3-5).

Although most Christians have interpreted these verses as something we are to do for ourselves, which is also appropriate, the context is certainly that of spiritual warfare for others, as clarified by *The Living Bible*. While reading this paraphrase, please especially notice the references and inferences to the root of pride and its cousin, rebellion. You will be encouraged by the absoluteness of the promises.

It is true that I am an ordinary, weak human being, but I don't use human plans and methods to win my battles. I use God's mighty weapons, not those made by men, to knock down the devil's strongholds. These weapons can break down every proud argument against God and every wall that can be built to keep men from finding Him. With these weapons I can capture rebels and bring them back to God, and change them into men whose hearts' desire is obedience to Christ (2 Cor. 10:3-5, *TLB*).

Let's take a deeper look at what God says here about how to deal with this skunk. Knowing that we often overlook the obvious, God first of all clearly states that our weapons of warfare are not human. We will never win people to Christ on an intellectual basis, nor will we do it through innovative techniques or methods alone. Certainly, a continual barrage of nagging and harassing questions won't bring them to the Lord.

Christian author Quin Sherrer sees the problem clearly when she states:

I've talked with many women who believed it was their responsibility to do everything in their power to "make" their husbands become Christians, but by their manipulative scheming, they only succeeded in turning their husbands away from any interest in spiritual matters. As many wives have learned the hard way, only the Holy Spirit can reveal to an individual the truth of who Jesus is (see John 16:8-13).[8]

Though continued pleading and nagging doesn't often work, sometimes we talk people into a salvation prayer without a true revelation (unveiling), but there is usually no real change because there is no true biblical repentance, which only comes from biblical revelation. When we approach people on a human basis, especially if they feel we are pressuring them, we generally make things worse. The root of pride in them rises up and defends itself, saying essentially, *I don't want anyone else controlling me or telling me what to do.* The irony is that if we attack this pride on a human level, we will only strengthen it.

God's Armory for Breaking Human Pride

However, if we would only realize it, we do have weapons that are "divinely powerful." God says, "Instead of using yours, I'll let you use Mine. Yours won't work; Mine will." *Dunatos,* one of the New Testament Greek words for miracle, is the word translated "powerful."[9] These weapons empowered by God will work miracles. The word is also translated "possible." Do you know anyone who seems impossible to reach? Will it take a miracle? With this power, their salvation is possible.

Paul Billheimer, a twentieth-century authority on prayer and author of *Destined for the Throne,* said his own salvation resulted from spiritual warfare waged on his behalf. He explains:

My mother used these weapons on me. I was as hostile to God as any sinner. I was fighting with all my might. But the time came when it was easier to lay down my arms of rebellion than to continue my resistance. The pressure exerted upon me by the Holy Spirit became so powerful that I voluntarily sought relief by yielding my rebellious will. The wooing of divine love was so strong that of my own free will I fell into the arms of redeeming grace. I became a willing "captive."[10]

What are these weapons we use in our warfare?

1. • _All forms of prayer._ Ephesians 6:18 mentions prayer in the context of the warfare we're in: "With all prayer and petition pray at all times in the Spirit, and with this in view, be on the alert with all perseverance and petition for all the saints." This would include supplication, agreement with other Christians, travail, praying in the Spirit, binding and loosing—any biblical form of prayer.

2. • _Praise._ Psalm 149:5-9 is a powerful reference to how God uses our praise of Him as a weapon. "Let the godly ones exult in glory; let them sing for joy on their beds. Let the high praises of God be in their mouth, and a two-edged sword in their hand" (vv. 5,6). Always praise God for the salvation of the one(s) for whom you are praying.

③ *The Word of God.* Ephesians 6:17: "And take the helmet of salvation, and the sword of the Spirit, which is the word of God." Speaking Scriptures that apply to your situation releases great power against the enemy. Jesus demonstrated this when He was confronted by Satan in the wilderness (see Matt. 4; Luke 4).

④ • *The name of Jesus.* Mark 16:17 states, "And these signs will accompany those who have believed: in My name they will cast out demons, they will speak with new tongues." Though praying in the name of Jesus is our access to the Father, it is also a powerful weapon against demonic powers and strongholds. Luke 10:17 tells us demons were subject to the disciples in Christ's name.

One of the things these weapons will help produce is enlightenment in the unbeliever. The word "light" in 2 Corinthians 4:4 is translated from the Greek word *photismos*, which means "illumination."[11] It is related to another word in Ephesians 1:18, "enlightened," which is translated from the word *photizo*—"to let in light,"[12] and is similar in meaning to revelation, or "lifting the veil." It is easy to see the English words "photo" or "photograph" in these words, and, indeed, they are derived from them.

What happens when one takes a photo? The shutter on the camera opens, letting in light, which brings an image. If the shutter on the camera does not open, there will be no image or picture regardless of how beautiful the scenery or elaborate the setting.

The same is true in the souls of human beings. And this is exactly what is being communicated—in photography language, as it were—in 2 Corinthians 4. It makes no difference how glorious our Jesus or how wonderful our message. If the veil (shutter) is not removed, there will be no true image (picture) of Christ.

In *The Trivialization of God*, Donald McCullough quotes Freeman Patterson, noted Canadian photographer, describing barriers that prevented him from seeing the best photo possibilities:

> Letting go of the self is an essential precondition to real seeing. When you let go of yourself, you abandon any preconceptions about the subject matter which might cramp you into photographing in a certain predetermined way.
>
> When you let go, new conceptions arise from your direct experience of the subject matter, and new ideas and feelings will guide you as you make pictures.[13]

What an appropriate phrase, "letting go of the self." In the same way that a photographer must remove barriers and see things differently, so must the sinner. If not, the picture of Christ is inferior at best.

We must ask God to lift the veil from unbelievers' spiritual eyes. Ask Him for enlightenment to come to the one for whom you are praying. Paul prayed for the Ephesians:

That the God of our Lord Jesus Christ, the Father of glory, may give to you a spirit of wisdom and of revelation in the knowledge of Him. I pray that the eyes of your heart may be enlightened, so that you may know what is the hope of His calling, what are the riches of the glory of His inheritance in the saints (Eph. 1:17,18).

If these Ephesians, already born again, needed revelation and enlightenment to grow in Christ, how much more must it happen for the unbeliever! Ask for it.

Information Versus Revelation

This brings us to a very important point. We need to understand the difference between *information* and *revelation*. Information is of the mind. However, biblical revelation, which involves and affects the mind, originates from the heart. Spiritual power is only released through revelation knowledge. The written word (*graphe*)[14] must become the living word (*logos*).[15] Even as believers, we must not just read, but abide or meditate in the Word, praying as the psalmist: "Open my eyes, that I may behold wonderful things from Thy law" (Ps. 119:18). The word "open," *galah*, also means "unveil or uncover"[16]—revelation.

Information can come immediately, but revelation is normally a process. As the parable of the sower demonstrates, all biblical truth comes in seed form. Early in my walk with the Lord, I was frustrated because the wonderful truths I had heard from some outstanding teachers were not working for me. When I heard the teachings, they had seemed powerful to me. I left the meetings saying, "I will never be the same!" But a few weeks and months later, I was the same.

As I complained to God and questioned the truth of what I had heard, the Lord spoke words to me that have radically changed my life: "Son, all truth comes to you in seed form. It may be fruit in the person sharing it, but it is seed to you. Whether or not it bears fruit depends on what you do with it. Spiritual information seeds must grow into fruit-producing revelation."

Knowledge or information alone, which is what humans have glorified and where they have begun their quest for meaning ever since the Fall, does not produce salvation. It does not necessarily lead to a true knowledge of God. Jesus said to the Pharisees, "You search the Scriptures, because you think that in them you have eternal life; and it is these that bear witness of Me" (John 5:39). He said to them on another occasion, "You plan to kill me, because My word has no entrance (makes no progress, does not find any place) in you" (John 8:37, *AMP*).

The Pharisees knew the Scriptures (*graphe*) probably better than you or I, but they did not know God. Information from the Word had not progressed to revelation. Many theologians today know the Scriptures thoroughly but don't know God well. Some, perhaps, do not know Him at all. They couldn't sit quietly in His presence for two hours without being bored silly. They have much information but little or no revelation. Revelation makes the Scriptures "spirit" and "life" (John 6:63). It makes them live.

Satan has an ability to dull the unbeliever's thinking where the gospel is concerned.

Why is this so important? Because we are forever short-circuiting God's process and, in so doing, short-circuiting the results. It is only revelation that leads to biblical faith and true change. Without it we are simply appealing to a fallen, selfish, humanistic mind created at the Fall that is always asking, "What's in it for me?" When we appeal to this mentality through human wisdom and intellect alone, we often preach a humanistic "What's in it for them?" gospel, and we produce—at best—humanistic, self-centered converts.

If, on the other hand, we preach a pure gospel, including repentance and the laying down of a person's own life (lordship of Christ), unbelievers are sure to reject it *unless* they receive a biblical revelation. In fact, our gospel often sounds ridiculous or moronic to them: "But a natural man does not accept the things of the Spirit of God; for they are foolishness to him, and he cannot understand them, because they are spiritually appraised" (1 Cor. 2:14). The word "foolishness" is *moria*, from which we get the word "moron."[17] What is the solution? *We must allow the Holy Spirit time to birth true repentance in unbelievers through God-given revelation.*

Revelation Backed with the Fire Power of Prayer

As we have stated, we must ask God to bring this revelation to the unbeliever. The hearing of the gospel isn't enough; prayer must accompany it.

- Pray that the person's heart be prepared, so that it will be "good soil" for the seed (Mark 4:8).
- Pray that Satan not be able to steal the seeds of truth (see Mark 4:15), and that nothing else will be able to destroy the seeds (see Mark 4:16-19).
- Pray that the Word becomes revelation through the lifting of the veil (see 2 Cor. 4:3,4). An excellent verse to use in prayer is Ephesians 1:17: "That the God of our Lord Jesus Christ, the Father of glory, may give to you a spirit of wisdom and of revelation in the knowledge of Him."
- Pray that the root of pride in them be broken (see 2 Cor. 10:3-5).
- Pray that the person comes to true repentance (see 2 Pet. 3:9). Second Timothy 2:25,26 is a wonderful passage to pray over individuals in this regard: "God may grant them repentance leading to the

knowledge of the truth, and they may come to their senses and escape from the snare of the devil, having been held captive by him to do his will."

Repentance does not mean to "turn and go another way." That change of direction is the *result* of repentance, not repentance itself, and is taken from the Greek word *epistrepho*, which is often translated "converted" or "turn."[18] Repentance—*metanoia*—means to have "a new knowledge or understanding"[19]—a change of mind. In biblical contexts, repentance is a new understanding that comes from God through an unveiling (revelation) and results in a new direction or lifestyle. It is necessary because of the turning to our own knowledge or understanding at the Fall.

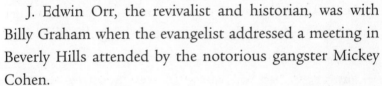

J. Edwin Orr, the revivalist and historian, was with Billy Graham when the evangelist addressed a meeting in Beverly Hills attended by the notorious gangster Mickey Cohen.

"He expressed some interest in the message," Orr later wrote, "so several of us talked with him, including Dr. Graham, but he made no commitment until some time later when another friend urged him—with Revelation 3:20 as a warrant—to invite Jesus Christ into his life.

"This he professed to do, but his life subsequently gave no evidence of repentance, 'the mighty change of mind, heart and life.' He rebuked our friend, telling him, 'You did not tell me that I would have to give up my work!' He meant his rackets. 'You did not tell me that I would have to give up my friends!' He meant his gangster associates.

"He had heard that so-and-so was a Christian cowboy, so-and-so was a Christian actress, so-and-so was a Christian senator, and he really thought he could be a Christian gangster.

"The fact is," said Orr, drawing the lesson, "repentance is the missing note in much modern evangelism."[20]

This "missing note in much modern evangelism"—biblical repentance—would produce God-centered Christians, not self-centered ones. It is the reversing of the effects of the Fall through Adam. Humanity chose their own wisdom, their own knowledge of good and evil, right and wrong. Humanity now needs "a new knowledge from God." Paul said in Acts 26:18 he was called "to open their eyes"—enlightenment, unveiling, revelation, repentance—"*so that* they may turn (*epistrepho*) from darkness to light" (emphasis added).

We help to create this "new knowledge" (repentance) through intercession. Our prayers play a part in the lifting of the veil (revelation) and the opening of the shutter (enlightenment).

Some dear friends of mine, Mell and Paula Winger, have seen many family members come to Christ as they have faithfully interceded for them through the years. The testimony regarding Paula's younger brother is especially powerful:

Doug Giles had an extremely ungodly lifestyle and was living in total rebellion. He hated the gospel message and was so repelled by our faith in Christ that he would leave the house when we came for dinner. We began devoting one night each week to pray and fast for Doug's salvation. We did this weekly for a year and a half, praying that he would be able to see the truth of the gospel, binding the spirit of rebellion that was controlling him and asking God to soften his heart so that he might be drawn to Him. Then, although we were no longer setting aside every Monday night to intercede for him, we continued to pray these and other principles for Doug during the next six years. Finally, one night while attending a Christian concert, he received Christ as his Savior. That was 17 years ago, and today Doug has a powerful evangelistic ministry based out of Miami, Florida.

I have heard Doug minister, and I can attest to the ministry he has. God is no respecter of persons—what He did through the prayer of Mell and Paula, He will do through yours.

QUESTIONS FOR WISDOM AND FAITH

1. If God is the one who draws people to Him, why is it important to be strategic in how we share the gospel?

2. What are the various kinds of veils (filters) that hinder people from accepting Christ as Lord? In your opinion, what is the most difficult veil that clouds the heart and mind?

3. Does sharing Scripture make people hard of heart, or does it break through their defenses and reservations?

4. Can believers (even acting in a sincere manner) hinder someone from entering the Kingdom by what they say and do?

Spiritual Warfare for the Lost

When Eileen from Baton Rouge heard me teach on "Spiritual Warfare for the Lost," she knew it was for her. She had been saved for 21 years and had been praying for her father for 26 years with no results. He had been raised in an occult atmosphere and was a hardened military man who never responded in any way to her many and varied attempts to reach him with the gospel.

She went home from the conference where she had heard me teach, pulled out her notes and began to diligently follow them in praying for her father. She also called her mother, gave her a condensed version of my teaching and told her there was a window of opportunity where he would be able to hear and respond. Four days before he died, her father prayed and accepted the Lord as his Savior.

Eileen went on to say,

I couldn't really celebrate Thanksgiving this year until I called and thanked you for sharing this teaching that showed me how to effectively pray for my dad with eternal results. I also shared this with our church, and several people came to me afterwards saying they now have hope to pray again. I wanted you to know that your teaching is having domino effects and impacting the lives of many. Thank you!

ASSAULTING STRONGHOLDS OF MIND AND HEART

There is an absolute connection between spiritual warfare

and intercession, especially in regards to praying for the lost. As we stated in the previous chapter, we have a role in removing the veil that blinds their minds. Part of the veil that blinds unbelievers is the strongholds referred to in 2 Corinthians 10:4: "For the weapons of our warfare are not carnal, but mighty through God to the pulling down of strongholds" (*KJV*). The *New American Standard Bible* states it this way: "For the weapons of our warfare are not of the flesh, but divinely powerful for the destruction of fortresses." The word "stronghold" is translated from the Greek word *ochuroma*, coming from the root word *echo*, which means "to have or hold."[1] This word for "stronghold" (*KJV*) or "fortress" (*NASB*) is literally a place from which to *hold* something *strongly*. It is also the word for a fort, a castle or a prison. Strongholds are not demons; they are places from which demons rule.

In essence, Satan has a place of strength *within* unbelievers from which he can imprison or hold on to them strongly. They are prisoners, captives, slaves. Christ was sent "to proclaim release to the *captives*" (Luke 4:18, emphasis added). We participate in the destruction of these "prisons" through spiritual warfare. What happened for Eileen and her father can happen for you.

I love the concept embodied in the word "destruction," or as the *KJV* says, "pulling down." These words are translated from the Greek word, *kathairesis*. This important and powerful word has a couple of pertinent meanings. One of them is "to bring down with violence or demolish" something.[2] God's plan is for us to become demolition agents, violently tearing down Satan's strongholds.

I remember as a small child watching the destruction of an old brick school. I was fascinated as the huge cement ball, attached to a gigantic crane, was swung time after time into the building, crashing through walls and ceilings and bringing incredible destruction. I suppose this would be, in one sense, a viable picture of our warfare as we systematically—one divine blow at a time—work destruction on the strongholds of darkness. It truly does usually happen this way—a systematic, ongoing, one-blow-at-a-time war against Satan's strongholds.

Sooner or later there will be a mighty explosion in the spirit, a stronghold will crumble to the ground and people will fall to their knees.

Yet I saw another huge building in Dallas, Texas, demolished several years ago. This edifice was much larger than the school I had seen destroyed as a child. This one covered nearly an entire city block, or at least it seemed that way to me. The demolition crew didn't use a wrecking ball for this one. And it didn't take days—it took seconds. They used dynamite strategically placed by experts to demolish this major structure in less than 10 seconds.

Since the phrase "divinely powerful" is the word *dunatos*,[3] from which we get the English word "dynamite," I like to think that this, in some ways, can also be a picture of our intercession. Unlike a detonated physical building, we don't usually see the answer to our intercession within seconds—we may be strategically placing the dynamite of the Spirit for days, weeks or months. But every time we take up our spiritual weapons and use them against the strongholds of the enemy, we are placing our explosive charges in strategic places. And sooner or later the Holy Detonator of heaven is going to say "Enough!" There will be a mighty explosion in the spirit, a stronghold will crumble to the ground and people will fall to their knees. Consider this beautiful story:

> Ellen was a mother and widow who persistently prayed for her five children after she was left to rear them alone. When gathering them around their father's casket, she had prayed, "Lord, I don't have anything to give You except myself and these children, but we commit ourselves to You and trust You to take care of us."
>
> Hardships hit, but with her faith in God steadfast, she continually declared, "We're going to make it!" When the state welfare agent wanted to place one boy, Charles, in an orphanage to lighten her load, she refused. "We may not look like much, but we're going to make it," she announced stubbornly to the agent who came to the farm to get Charles.

Years passed. The children stayed true to the Lord, and most of them entered the ministry—all except one. When the middle boy, Melvin, joined the army, he fell into the ways of the world, married an unbeliever, and forsook the faith of his childhood. Ellen never stopped praying for her wayward son. Every time friends or family members lamented over Melvin's spiritual condition, she had a standard response: "God doesn't lie—I'll never stop believing. My boy's going to make it."

One day, Charles received word that his unsaved brother Melvin had died suddenly of a heart attack. He immediately flew to Boston and went directly to the funeral home. As he stood before his brother's casket, wondering how his mother would respond to the shocking news, Melvin's wife came into the room.

"Charles, I want to tell you something that happened last night that I think will make you feel better," she said. "I had gone to bed ahead of Melvin. A little later he went from room to room to tell all the children goodnight, then came to our bedroom. But instead of getting into bed, he did something I've never seen him do in all the years we've been married. He knelt beside the bed and began praying. Then I noticed he was praying in a strange language—a language I've never heard him speak before. After a little while he got into bed and went to sleep. Early this morning he had the heart attack and died."

His fears relieved, Charles phoned his mother's home and recounted the story. "Well, Mom, what do you think?" he asked.

Strong and confident, her voice came back so real he could almost see her Irish eyes sparkling. "I think my boy made it!" Ellen said triumphantly.[4]

The one you are praying for is going to make it, as well. God is going to show you just how to pray so that you can demolish every part of Satan's fortress.

"We are destroying speculations and every lofty thing raised up against the knowledge of God, and we are taking every thought captive to the obedience of Christ" (2 Cor. 10:5). Verse 4 says our divinely empowered weapons are for the destruction or demolition of strongholds, and verse 5 elaborates more fully on just what comprises the strongholds we're going to demolish. In other words, the Holy Spirit breaks down for us exactly what the stronghold or prison is made of. This is critical information as we begin to war for the lost.

Breaking the Foundations of Resistance
Specifically, He shares with us three major components of the fortress or prison. These are the things we will begin to call out in prayer and demolish as we war over individuals with our divinely empowered weapons.

The first aspect of the stronghold He mentions is "speculations"—*logismos* (plural *logismoi*). This word speaks not of the scattered individual thoughts of humans but of their calculative reasoning, their wisdom or logic.[5] Our word "logic" is actually derived from this Greek root. *Logismos* is the sum total of the accumulated wisdom and information learned over time. It becomes what one really believes—the person's mind-set. The Moffatt translation calls them "theories." Humanity, before the Fall, got their wisdom and logic—their beliefs—from God. Now James 3:15 tells us they come from the earth, the soul or intellect and demons.

The word *logismos* includes philosophies (conscious or unconscious), religions, humanism, atheism, Hinduism, Buddhism, Islam, racism, intellectualism, Judaism, materialism, roots of rejection, perversions, alcoholism, other addictions—anything that causes a person to think a certain way.

> One mom travailed in prayer for some time about her drug-addicted daughter. One evening while lying on her face in prayer, she heard the Lord's quiet voice promising that [her daughter would] soon be set free. Wiping her tears, that mom got up and began praising God. She continued praising God for victory, though there was no outward change in her daughter. Five long months passed. Then, when the daughter overdosed, she was ready for help. After some Christian counseling, she was set free.[6]

Though there were no doubt other *logismoi* in this daughter, one was drug addiction, which controlled her thinking.

How does a *logismos* blind an individual? How do they veil truth? The way the human mind functions dictates that when people hear the gospel, before they even have time to think or reason about what they are hearing, it is filtered through the subconscious or memory where all other information—including these *logismoi*—is stored. This means that unbelievers don't hear only what we are saying, they hear what we are saying *plus* what they already believe.

In the past, before realizing the distorted perception of the unbeliever, I often wondered why people could hear and reject powerful gospel presentations. Now I understand that what the unbelievers heard was filtered through a belief system—a veil—that caused them to hear something totally different. When "hearing" the gospel message, they didn't hear what I heard, see what I saw or understand what I understood. The fourth verse of 2 Corinthians 4 clearly states this: "that they might not *see* the light of the gospel of the glory of Christ, who is the *image* of God" (emphasis added). They simply do not see the same image of Christ that we do. To clearly see Him is to love and want Him.

In his novel *My Lovely Enemy*, Canadian Mennonite author Rudy Wiebe aptly pictures how different the same thing looks to different people:

> It could be like standing on your head in order to see the world clearer. . . . If one morning you began walking on your hands, the whole world would be hanging. The trees, these ugly brick and tile buildings wouldn't be fixed here so solid and reassuring; they'd be pendant. The more safe and reliable they seem now, the more helpless they'd be then.[7]

The same world would look very different, depending on the way it was seen. The same is true with the message of Jesus Christ. People's *logismoi* distort, color or turn upside down their perceptions of the gospel message.

For example, I was sharing the gospel with a girl who had been horribly abused. "God is love," I said. "He loves you so much He sent His Son to die for you." She heard more than what I said. I know because she said to me, "Oh? If He is love, why would He have allowed me to be so abused? Doesn't sound like a loving God to me." That is a *logismos*—a belief, a philosophy, her wisdom, her logic. Someone will need to intercede for her and help tear down the *logismos* with "divinely powerful" weapons. The Holy Spirit will need to remove that veil, allowing her to see clearly.

On another occasion, I was sharing the gospel with a fellow who had a *logismos* I call "good-ol'-boy-ism." He was just too nice a guy to think he needed saving. "I'm a pretty good guy," he said. "I don't cheat on my wife, beat my kids, lie, curse or steal. I don't think God would send me to hell." His *logismos*, or belief system, was that a person can be good enough to get to heaven.

How does the gospel break through these arguments? Certainly the gospel of truth itself has power to break down some of this when anointed by the Holy Spirit. But it usually takes a long period of time—if you can get them to listen. It is much wiser to plow the ground ahead of time, preparing for the reception of the seed by pulling down these strongholds, as George Müller and his team did for orphans in their care.

The spiritual condition of the orphans generally brought great sorrow to our hearts, because there were so few among them who were in earnest about their souls and resting on the atoning death of the Lord Jesus for salvation. Our sorrow led us to lay it on the whole staff of assistants, matrons and teachers to seek earnestly for the Lord's blessing on the souls of the children. This was done in our united prayer meetings and, I have reason to believe, in secret sessions of prayer as well.

In the year 1872, in answer to and as a result of our private and united prayers, there were more believers by far among the orphans than ever. On January 8, 1872, the Lord began to work among them, and this work continued more or less afterward.

At the end of July 1872, I received the statements of all the matrons and teachers in the five houses, who reported to me that, after careful observation and conversation, they had good reason to believe that 729 of the orphans then under our care were believers in the Lord Jesus. This number of believing orphans was by far greater than we had ever had before, for which we adore and praise the Lord![8]

Perhaps you already know what these *logismoi* are in the person for whom you are praying. If not, ask the Holy Spirit to reveal them to you. He will. And when He does, call them by name, quoting 2 Corinthians 10:3-5. Say, "In the name of the Lord Jesus Christ I am destroying you, stronghold of . . ." Do it daily until the person comes to Christ.

> During Operation Desert Storm, the Iraqi war machine was overwhelmed by the Coalition Forces' ability to strike strategic targets with never-seen-before accuracy. Unknown to the Iraqis, the Allied Supreme Command had dropped Special Operations Forces (SOF) deep behind enemy lines. These men provided bombing coordinates for military targets and firsthand reports on the effectiveness of subsequent bombing missions.
>
> To avoid unintended targets, pinpoint bombing was often required. A soldier from a SOF unit standing on the ground would request an aircraft high overhead to drop a laser-guided missile. Using a handheld laser, the soldier would point at the target. The missile would hone in on the soldier's target for the hit.[9]

In much the same way, our prayers focus the attention of God's powerful weapons on the *logismos* fortresses of Satan in the minds of unbelievers.

The second part of the stronghold we must demolish is "every lofty thing raised up against the knowledge of God." I like using the *KJV* for this verse because it uses "high thing" to translate the Greek word *hupsoma*, which is actually the same root word for "Most High" God. It actually means "any elevated place or thing."[10] This is referring to the same root of pride we discovered hidden in the word "blinded" in 2 Corinthians 4:3,4. It is the "most highness" that came to humanity at the Fall when Adam and Eve bought the lie, "You will be like God" (Gen. 3:5).

By disobeying God, humankind, like Satan, exalted themselves to a place of equality with the Most High. We became, however, not the Most High but our own most high, filled with pride. One leading lexicon even defined *hupsoma* as "all pride that rises up."[11] The word would then encompass all mind-sets that exalt themselves against the knowledge of God. It involves a desire to rule our own lives, decide for ourselves right and wrong and basically be our own god.

The good news is that we can also tear down this stronghold in people through spiritual warfare so they can humble themselves and bow their knees to Christ. An example of this power is seen below:

Darlene's husband died of a heart attack and her older son was killed by a highway sniper—both within one year. Sean, her only remaining child, moved back home to help her with their struggling family business.

Darlene soon realized with dismay that Sean had strayed far from the Lord he had once served. He never read his Bible or went to church, and he was very cold in his attitude toward her.

"Stay out of my room," he barked at her one day when she had gone into his room for something. "I'll take care of my things in there."

To keep peace, Darlene tried to leave Sean to himself. But many nights she walked the floor praying for her son, pleading with God to intervene in his life. One day she went into his room to get dirty laundry and found a marijuana plant growing under a special light he'd rigged in the closet.

Standing there, getting more and more angry at the devil, she screamed at the plant. "Die, in the name of Jesus! I curse you and forbid you to live in this house."

The next day the plant was dead.

That night as she again walked the floor praying for Sean, she felt the Holy Spirit leading her to pray, *Lord, I give You my son. Give me back a brother in the Lord.*

From then on her prayers changed. She began to praise the Lord that Sean was going to become a brother in the Lord to her. She stopped begging God but continued to thank Him for the work He would do in Sean's life.

Two weeks later, her son came in early on a Saturday night. He knew Darlene always had a prayer meeting and Bible study going on then. Finding the Bible teacher and his wife still there, Sean began querying them. Before the night was over, Sean asked for God's forgiveness and promised to follow Jesus for the rest of his life.

"God did give me a brother in the Lord," Darlene said, rejoicing. "Almost ten years have passed, and Sean is still walking with the Lord."[12]

The pride in this young man's life—his desire to rebel against authority and rule his own life—was torn down, demolished through intercession.

Read 2 Corinthians 10:5 again, this time from *The Living Bible*:

> These weapons can break down every proud argument against God and every wall that can be built to keep men from finding Him. With these weapons I can capture rebels and bring them back to God, and change them into men whose hearts' desire is obedience to Christ.

I like the "cans" and "everys" in this verse. The Lord doesn't wish us luck or tell us that we will win a few once in awhile. He lets us know we can break down every proud argument and every wall; we can capture rebels! And we must!

With this in mind, consider the third aspect of strongholds. The Lord tells us we can take "every thought captive to the obedience of Christ." The word "thought" is *noema*, which also means plans, schemes, devices or plots.[13] It refers to the spontaneous thoughts and temptations Satan uses to assault the unbelievers, as well as the schemes and plans he uses to keep them in darkness. In intercession we must declare boldly that *no weapon* of Satan's will prosper. We must bind his plans and stand against them through prayer. We can and should pray that the unbeliever be shielded from Satan's thoughts and temptations.

Never stop praying for "hopeless" cases, for no one is beyond the Lord's ability to convict and convert. Consider the example of E. Howard Cadle. His mother was a Christian, but his father was an alcoholic. Cadle began emulating his father, drinking and out of control, and soon was in the clutches of the crime syndicate.

Every night at eight o'clock, his mother knelt by his bed praying. One evening, Cadle pulled a gun on a man and squeezed the trigger, but the weapon never fired and was quickly knocked away. Cadle noticed that it was exactly eight o'clock, and somehow he'd been spared from committing murder.

He continued headlong in vice, however, and his health deteriorated to where the doctor told him he had only six months to live. Dragging himself home, penniless and pitiful, he collapsed in his mother's arms, saying, "Mother, I've broken your heart. I'd like to be saved, but I've sinned too much."

The elderly woman opened her Bible and read Isaiah 1:18: *"Though your sins are like scarlet, they shall be as white as snow."* That morning, March 14, 1914, Cadle started life anew. The change in him was dramatic and permanent.

With Christ now in his heart, he turned his con skills into honest pursuits and started making money, giving 75 percent of it to the Lord's work. He helped finance crusades in which thousands were converted and became one of America's earliest and most popular radio evangelists.

He once said: "Until He calls me, I shall preach the same gospel that caused my mother to pray for me. And when I have preached my last sermon, I want to sit at His feet and say, 'Thank You, Jesus, for saving me.'"[14]

Like Mrs. Cadle, we can turn unbelievers "from darkness to light and from the dominion of Satan to God" (Acts 26:18). We are called to enforce and make effectual the freedom Christ procured.

The unbeliever cannot war for himself. He cannot and will not overcome the strongholds of darkness, and he will not understand the gospel until the veil lifts. We must take our divinely dynamic weapons and fight. The powers of darkness will resist, but "do not be afraid of them, remember the Lord who is great and awesome, and fight for your brothers, your sons, your daughters, your wives, and your houses" (Neh. 4:14).

QUESTIONS FOR WISDOM AND FAITH

1. What philosophy *(logismoi)* is the most subtle in affecting nonbelievers today? Can such a philosophy affect a Christian, too?

2. What aspect of pride *(hupsoma)* hindered you from becoming a follower of Christ? Why?

3. What does it mean to capture a thought *(noema)* to the obedience of Christ? Is that self-discipline? What thoughts in your life need to be taken captive?

4. What kinds of spiritual fruit (see Gal. 5) come from our laboring and wrestling for the salvation of others through prayer?

Bearing God's Heartbreaking Burdens

The Lord does and will give His people a taste of His own long-suffering heart and His desire that all should come to know Him. Consider this story:

John "Praying" Hyde grew up hearing his father, a minister, often mention the needs of overseas mission fields and praying for laborers to be sent forth. At McCormick Theological Seminary, John committed himself to foreign evangelism and, following graduation, he sailed for Bombay.

Initially overcome by the difficulties of climate and language, John preached from village to village but grew discouraged as there were few converts. Then he discovered Isaiah 62:6,7, which became his personal motto. He began praying with remarkable intensity—missing meals, meetings and preaching appointments. As he spent days and nights in prayer, revival began to come down upon his labors in India.

At the beginning of 1908, he prayed earnestly to win at least one soul to Christ every day. By December 31, he had recorded over four hundred converts. The following year, the Lord laid two souls per day on his heart, and his prayer was again answered. The next year he prayed for four souls daily with similar results.

Once, stopping at a cottage for water, Praying Hyde pleaded with God for ten souls. He presented the gospel to the family, and, by the end of his visit, all nine members of the family had been saved. But what of number ten? Suddenly a nephew who had been outside ran into the room and was promptly converted.

Hyde's great missionary work flowed from his prayer life like water from a faucet, and he finally wore himself out in prayer, staying on his knees, night after night, year after year, reminding God of his promises and giving the Lord no rest. The great prayer warrior died on February 17, 1912, his last words being: *Bol, Visu Masih, Ki Jah*—"Shout the victory of Jesus Christ!"[1]

I don't necessarily want you to "wear yourself out in prayer" to the point of death, as some say Praying Hyde did, but I do want to talk to you about passion . . . tears . . . allowing God's heart to be born in and released from you.

THE PASSION TO PRAY

At the risk of sounding self-serving, or perhaps even prideful, I want to share a little more with you about my experience of October 4, 2000, when God moved upon me for America. I do so cautiously and somewhat hesitantly because the time was very personal and precious. But perhaps it will help us understand some things I consider very important.

God had moved upon me very powerfully during the worship that evening, but not with tears or intercession. It was a wonderful intimacy that, paradoxically, became mixed with a sense of foreboding or heaviness. Not until one of my associates articulated a burden for the elections, warning of the intense warfare surrounding it and its outcome so precariously hanging in the balance, did I realize what God was placing on me.

Intending to go ahead and deliver my message, I walked to the podium. As I opened my Bible, what I can only describe as a wave of God's presence overwhelmed me in a matter of seconds. I explained to our congregation that I didn't know exactly what was happening, but that I knew I couldn't speak. The wave continued and within seconds I was weeping uncontrollably. Thus began three and a half hours of deep intercession for America, specifically for the upcoming presidential election.

By the time the evening was over, I knew several things:

1. This was to be the most important election in decades. God had brought the nation to a point where the spiritual decline of the last 30 to 40 years could begin to turn. If the opportunity wasn't seized now, however, it would take decades before it would be available again.
2. This would only take place if God's person was elected. (Not that our faith should ever be in a person or political party, but God can work through some people and not others. For example, he had to remove King Saul and appoint David, a man after God's heart, to lead Israel).
3. If the election were held at that moment, God's person would not win.

4. God was NOT going to change this and give us His choice without the prayers and repentance from the Body of Christ. He wouldn't do it in spite of us; He would only do it *through* us—if there were enough prayers and a true repentance in the Church of America.

5. I didn't know what "enough" was. I only knew I had to issue the call to pray.

God graciously anointed the prayer alert we issued and within days a massive prayer movement was underway. Of course, as the election unfolded, the degree of the warfare became obvious. Not only an election but the future of a nation hung in the balance.

I, and many others, carried this burden of the Lord from early October until the day Vice President Gore conceded. For me, it was overwhelming at times. I wept often. Though it may sound strange, occasionally I would drape the American flag around me and pray for hours again, often with many tears. I sometimes felt—though I knew I was one of many—that I was carrying the weight of a nation on my shoulders.

At one point I asked God to remove the burden. It was becoming too unbearable; emotionally I was becoming overwhelmed. I knew the future of America was being determined: a harvest of millions, a generation of youth, millions of unborn babies, even millions of unsaved people from around the world would be affected by what happened.

God did not remove the burden, but He did give me grace and understanding to carry it. He showed me how to do it from my heart by the power of the Holy Spirit, and not from my mind and emotions. It was still heavy and at times emotional, but I was walking in the Spirit, not my own strength, and could therefore endure it. I am fully convinced that our prayers—those of the Body of Christ—determined the outcome of the election.

Bearing a Measure of God's Burden

Why have I shared this? To help explain the power of tears, of passion, of allowing God to touch us with His heart so He can pray through us. When Nehemiah heard the spiritual condition of his nation, Israel, he "sat down and wept and mourned for days" (Neh. 1:4). Ezra did as well, "weeping and prostrating himself before the house of God" and others "wept bitterly" with Ezra (Ezra 10:1). Both situations resulted in breakthroughs. *There are times when only God's passionate heart, released through us, will produce the needed results.* Charles Finney relates the following story:

A minister once related a story to me about a town that had not had a revival in many years. The Church was nearly extinct, the youth were all unconverted and desolation reigned unbroken. There lived, in a retired part of the town, an aged blacksmith who stammered so badly that it was painful to hear him speak. One Friday, as he worked in his shop, alone, he became very upset about the state of the Church and of the impenitent. His agony became so great that he had to put away his work, lock the shop door, and spend the afternoon in prayer.

He continued to pray all day. Then he asked his minister to arrange a conference meeting. After some hesitation, the minister consented, even though he feared few people would attend. He called the meeting the same evening at a large private house. When evening came, more people assembled than could be accommodated in the house. All were silent for a time, until one sinner broke out in tears and said, "If anyone could pray, would he pray for me?" Another followed, and another, and still another, until people from every part of town were under deep conviction. It was also remarkable that they all dated their conviction to the hour the old man prayed in his shop. A powerful revival followed. Thus this stammering old man's prayer prevailed, and as a prince, he had power with God.[2]

By sharing this story, as well as what transpired with me, I run the risk of making you feel that if you're not weeping for someone's salvation, your prayers won't be effective. Please don't interpret what I'm saying in this way. My spiritual passion isn't always released through tears, nor will yours be; there are many biblical ways to pray and to release our faith. In fact, most of the time, my intercession does not involve tears.

What I am saying is that we must allow ourselves to receive the burden of the Lord. We must let His heart for people become ours, so much so that when we pray, it is really Him praying through us.

The apostle Paul wrote to the Corinthian believers and said that God "gave us the ministry of reconciliation, namely, that God was in Christ reconciling the world to Himself, not counting their trespasses against them, and

If we let Him, the Holy Spirit will help us in prayer by allowing us to partake of His compassion for the lost.

He has committed to us the word of reconciliation. Therefore, we are ambassadors for Christ, *as though God were entreating through us; we beg you on behalf of Christ,* be reconciled to God" (2 Cor. 5:18-20, emphasis added). Paul used strong words: "entreating" and "beg." Yet he said, in essence, that he was actually doing it for God.

Just a couple of verses later in 2 Corinthians 6:1, he uses the phrase "working together with Him." Romans 8:26 says God "helps" us in our intercession. The word is *sunantilambanomai,* which means "to take hold of together with against." If we let Him, the Holy Spirit will help us in prayer by allowing us to partake of His compassion for the lost. Certainly this is one of the ways He takes hold with us in intercession.

The great Charles Finney said it this way:

> His prayers seem to flow from the intercessor's heart like water: "O LORD, revive Thy work" (Hab. 3:2). Sometimes this feeling is very deep. This is by no means enthusiasm. It is just what Paul felt when he said, "My little children, of whom I travail in birth" (Gal. 4:19). I do not mean to say that it is essential to have this great distress in order to have the spirit of prayer. But this deep, continual, earnest desire for the salvation of sinners is what constitutes the spirit of prayer for a revival.[3]

Passionate Caring

The following two passages on tears describe the passion of which Finney speaks. Interpret the tears, however, as passionate caring, not necessarily as literal tears, which is certainly the spirit of what God is saying. Psalm 126:5,6 states: "Those who sow in tears shall reap with joyful shouting. He who goes to and fro weeping, carrying his bag of seed, shall indeed come again with a shout of joy, bringing his sheaves with him."

Our tears are called seeds in these verses. In others words, God uses them to produce a harvest. The word for seed, *zera*, means not only "seed" or "crop" but also "offspring, progeny or family."[4] It's not that difficult to see the symbolism. God uses our "tear seeds" to bring forth His family!

Or perhaps we want to apply it to our family. Remember *zera*, the word for seed, also means family. When we weep in intercession (or remember, pray passionately) for our family, the prayer seeds (*zera*) we are sowing will grow into a family (*zera*) harvest! In other words, the seeds of intercession you sow will grow into saved children, spouses, parents, etc. That will be our harvest. Hallelujah!

Another great verse on tears is Psalm 56:8: "Thou hast taken account of my wanderings; put my tears in Thy bottle. Are they not in Thy book?" The bottle referred to here isn't just a storage container. It is the word *nodah*, meaning a skin used to transform juice to wine or cream to butter.[5] Again, God is trying to tell us our tears (or passionate prayers) will be transformed into something else. God will store them and *use* them, not *waste* them. And when He is finished, they will be changed into wine—fruitfulness. Where intercession for the lost is concerned, this fruit will be saved people.

Go ahead and become a person of passion. You cannot do so on your own, but the passionate God—the very passion that sent Him to the Cross—is in you. "Zeal for [His] house" (Ps. 69:9; John 2:17) is yours for the asking. This kind of passion is exemplified well in the following story:

Police don't know where Deborah Kemp found the strength, but she knows. Her six-year-old daughter, Ashleye, was in the back seat. Deborah had just finished putting gas in her car when a man attempted to steal her car. The thirty-four-year-old mother was dragged on her knees for several blocks as she clung to the door and steering wheel of the moving car. "I wasn't trying to be a hero," she said. "I was concerned about my baby . . . that was part of me in that car." Kemp eventually pulled the suspect from the car and beat him with an anti-theft club device while he apologized and begged her to stop. The driverless car went out of control and smashed into a restaurant, breaking a gas line. That's when the child woke up. Kemp suffered only ripped pants and bloody knees. The child was not injured. The suspect couldn't walk due to leg injuries he incurred.[6]

Passionless people change nothing. But people like Deborah Kemp, motivated by passionate love, refuse to allow Satan, the thief, to steal, kill and destroy God's "babies." Refuse to be lukewarm in your approach to lost souls. Be hot. Let His love constrain you (see 2 Cor. 5:14, *KJV*). He really does want to love through you.

He is waiting for you to ask.

QUESTIONS FOR WISDOM AND FAITH

1. Can we choose to accept God's heartache over certain people and events or does the Lord lay it upon us regardless?

2. Does bearing God's burdens entail feelings alone? Are we moved to reason, understand, and articulate more clearly what the burden is to ourselves and to others?

3. In some of our pleadings to God in prayer, does the Lord say "no" to our knocking?

4. How do we distinguish between what is God's burden for us to pray versus something that is our own personal burden? Or are they one and the same?

CHAPTER SIX

Labor-Intensive Realities

It's wonderful to see the overflow, or domino effect, that sometimes happens when we pray for family members. Lorraine's family is an example of this principle. For years she prayed for her brother Stuart and his family to come to Christ. His typical response was, "Don't bother me with talk about religion."

Then one day Stuart called to tell Lorraine that his son, Bart, was getting out of jail. "Can you and your husband help him find a place to stay?" Stuart asked. "The jail is not that far from where you live." Lorraine and her husband agreed to invite Bart to stay with them. After he moved into their upstairs bedroom, they learned that, while in jail, he had had an encounter with God. As a spiritually hungry new Christian, Bart became involved in a local church and began to work in a Christian ministry. As he grew in faith, he became eager for his father to also know Christ in an intimate way.

Lorraine knew that God was answering her prayers for Stuart when he agreed to attend a Christian men's rally with Bart and her husband. While there, Bart asked his dad if he would like to accept Christ as his Savior and Lord, and Stuart responded affirmatively. Lorraine's prayers of more than 40 years were answered when Bart led his own father in a salvation prayer.[1]

During her years of intercession for her brother, Lorraine probably never envisioned that Stuart would come to the

Lord through this sequence of events. But as a result of her prayers, this father and son were both brought to salvation in Christ.

GOD'S BIRTHERS

Prayer releases power from the Holy Spirit, which brings about the new birth or salvation. We are "birthers" for God. The Holy Spirit wants to bring forth spiritual sons and daughters through our intercession. Jesus said in John 7:38: "From his *innermost being* shall flow rivers of living water" (emphasis added). "Innermost being" is translated from the Greek word *koilia*, which means "womb."[2] We are the womb

All of us can and should regularly involve ourselves in intercession for the lost, realizing it will cause people to be born again.

of God upon the earth. We are not the source of life, but we are carriers of the source of life. We do not generate life; but we release, through prayer, Him who does. All of us can and should regularly involve ourselves in intercession for the lost, realizing it will cause people to be born again.

Please understand that we don't birth anything spiritually; the Holy Spirit does. He is the birthing agent of the Godhead (see Luke 1:34,35; John 3:3-8). He is the power source of the Godhead (see Luke 4:14,18; Acts 1:8; 10:38). He is the power behind Creation which, as we will see, is likened to a birthing (see Gen. 1). He is the one who supplies power to God's will, giving it life and substance. He gives birth to the will of God. He is the one who breathes God's life into people, bringing physical and spiritual life (see Gen. 2:7; Ezek. 37:9,10,14; Acts 2:1-4). Concerning salvation, we call this the new birth or the new creation. Anything we might accomplish in intercession that results in someone being born again would have to be because our prayers caused or released the Holy Spirit to do something.

For example, Elijah as a human being couldn't birth or produce rain. Yet, James 5:17,18 tells us that his prayers did. Paul couldn't birth through travailing prayer the new birth or maturity in the Galatians, yet Galatians 4:19 implies that his intercession did. We cannot produce spiritual sons and daughters through our human abilities, yet Isaiah 66:7,8 tells us that our travail can. If we cannot create or birth these things through our own power or ability, then it seems fairly obvious that our prayers must in some way cause or release the Holy Spirit to do so.

Ephesians 3:20,21 states:

Now to Him who is able to do exceeding abundantly beyond all that we ask or think, according to the power that works within us, to Him be the glory in the church and in Christ Jesus to all generations forever and ever. Amen.

The word for "exceeding abundantly beyond" is the same word for the abundant grace of God in Romans 5:20. The word is *huperperissos*. *Perissos* means "superabundant,"[3] *huper* means "beyond" or "more than."[4] Together, they would mean superabundantly with more added to that. That's like saying "more than more than." Ephesians 3:20 says He has enough power to do more than we can ask or think with more added to that—more than more than.

God's Womb—the Church

So, why are we often deficient? The power source is obviously not the problem. The rest of Ephesians 3:20 gives us a clue. It tells us He is going to do this more than more than enough "according to the power that works within us." Wuest translates the phrase "in the measure of the power which is operative in us." The word "measure" is *kata*, which not only contains the implication of that which is measured in us, but Strong says it is also used at times with the connotation of "distribution."[5] He is going to do this superabundantly more than we can ask or think in the measure of the power that is distributed from us.

There is literal power from the Holy Spirit that can be released from us. The power of God that brings life, healing and wholeness to the earth flows out from us—the Church. Please don't picture some throne in heaven and feel like that's the only place from which His power flows.

He has now made His throne in our hearts and we are the temple of the Holy Spirit. We are the *naos* of God. In 1 Corinthians 3:16 and 6:19 this word is used and literally means "holy of holies."[6] We are now the holy of holies, the dwelling place of God upon the earth. When He moves to release power upon the earth, it doesn't have to shoot out of the sky somewhere—it comes from His people where His Spirit dwells upon the earth. We, the Body of Christ, are God's womb from which His life is birthed or released upon the earth. The life that Christ produces flows from the womb of the Church.

Inducing Spiritual Labor

You must release through prayer the power of God inside of you on a consistent basis. James 5:16 (*KJV*) says, "The *effectual fervent* prayer of a righteous man availeth much" (emphasis added). Wuest translates it this way: "A prayer of a righteous person is able to do much as it operates." Notice the verse doesn't say, "A prayer of a righteous person is able to do much because it causes God to operate."

It certainly does this, but that's not what this verse is telling us. It says, "A prayer of a righteous person is able to do much as it—*the prayer*—operates" (emphasis added). The *Amplified* translation reads, "The earnest (heartfelt, continued) prayer of a righteous man makes tremendous power available [dynamic in its working]." The point is that our prayers release the power of the Holy Spirit to work. Notice the word "continued." The *Amplified* captures the present tense meaning of the verb. We do this continuously until we see results. We have the power inside of us that created the world—the same power that went into the depths of the earth and took the keys from the kingdom of darkness. We must release it, and we do so by prayer.

Rosy was the first person in her devout Buddhist family in China to receive Christ. The tradition in her family was for the parents to take her and her siblings to the temple every week. They paid the Buddhist priests to write prayers and predictions of good luck for each of the children. The papers containing these writings were burned at an altar; then the ashes were stirred up in water and the children had to drink the mixture. The parents did this thinking it would assure the safety and well-being of their children. "The truth is, we actually were ingesting demons every week," Rosy said.

Rosy first heard the gospel message at a youth camp when she was 18. She accepted the Lord as her Savior and began to eagerly study the Bible. She memorized Scripture and began praying for her immediate family to receive Christ. At first they completely rejected Rosy and her newfound faith, but as Rosy continued to release the power of the Holy Spirit through prayer, one by one they began responding to the gospel. During a period of several years, she led every family member to the Lord. For many years she and her husband have been in full-time ministry, mostly in Asia, and now their son is preparing to do missions work among Muslims.[7]

Rosy's continued intercession for her family is a wonderful example of how people can be loosed from the kingdom of darkness as the power of the Holy Spirit is released through prayer.

Understanding, then, that it is the Holy Spirit's power actually doing the work, I want to say unequivocally that *prayer releases the power of the Holy Spirit to bring about the new birth*. To demonstrate this, various Scriptures use the same words that describe what the Holy Spirit does in birthing or bringing forth life as are used to describe what our prayers accomplish.

Genesis 1:1,2 (*KJV*) says, "In the beginning . . . the earth was without form and void." The words "without form" are translated from the Hebrew word *tohuw*, which means "a desolation; to lie waste; a desert;"[8] "confusion;"[9] "empty (barren)."[10] Sounds like lost people to me (we'll make the connection shortly).

Verse 2 goes on to say, "The Spirit of God moved upon the face of the waters." The Hebrew word *rachaph*, which is translated "moved" in this verse, literally means "to brood over."[11] "Brood" comes from the root word "breed," which means to bring forth offspring. In fact, this phrase in the *Amplified* translation reads, "The Spirit of God was moving, hovering, *brooding* over the face of the waters" (emphasis added). In using this term to describe Creation, the Holy Spirit is using the analogy of birthing something. When the Holy Spirit brooded, or hovered, over the earth, He was releasing His creative power at the words of Jesus, giving birth to what Christ spoke.

Psalm 90:2 confirms this, actually calling what the Holy Spirit did at Creation a birthing when it uses two important Hebrew words: "Before the mountains were born (*yalad*), or Thou didst give birth to (*chuwl*) the earth and the world, even from everlasting to everlasting, Thou art God."

Although the words are not translated "travail" in this verse, *yalad* and *chuwl* are also the primary Hebrew words for travail. Each one is translated variously in the Old Testament: "bring forth," "born," "give birth to," "travail," among others (for examples see Deut. 32:18; Job 15:7; 39:1). Regardless of how they are translated, the concept is that of giving birth to something. It is not always referring to a literal, physical birth but is often used for the idea of creating. We do the same thing in our vocabulary. We might say an idea, vision or nation was born or conceived. We're obviously not speaking of a physical birth but of something new coming into being. In much the same way, Psalm 90:2 likens the Genesis account of Creation to a birthing.

Now, let's make the prayer connection. These are the very same words used in Isaiah 66:8: "As soon as Zion *travailed [chuwl]* she also *brought forth [yalad]* her sons." This is extremely important! What the Holy Spirit was doing in Genesis when He "brought forth" or "gave birth to" the earth and the world is exactly what He wants to do through our prayers in bringing forth spiritual sons and daughters. He wants to hover around (*tohuw*) lost, lifeless, confused, spiritually barren individuals, releasing His awesome power to convict, break bondages, bring revelation and draw them to Himself in order to cause the new birth or new creation in them. *Yes, the Holy Spirit wants to birth through our prayers!* And if He can do so to create all we see around us, He can certainly do it in the one for whom you are praying. Consider this story:

> When Pam gave her life back to the Lord, she felt compelled to take up the prayer mantle of her deceased mother and grandmother and intercede for her siblings. The five children had been raised by a godly mother who, as Pam says, "stood on the Word that promised if she taught them the way of the Lord, when they were old they would not depart from it. Mother and Grandmother prayed for years for this household."
>
> After their deaths, the children strayed far from the Lord, and Satan made his bid to trap them in the world. Of special concern was O'Brien, a brother who became drawn into relationships with unbelieving women. Then, while stationed in Asia, he married a Buddhist. Pam was heartbroken that he had rejected the Lord and embraced a false god instead.
>
> But Pam continued to pray, asking the Holy Spirit to hover around her brother and his wife—to break bondages, release revelation and draw them

to Himself. She asked God to also remember the many prayers of their grandmother and mother. Finally, after two years, she was overjoyed to receive O'Brien's phone call: "Sis, I want you to know I found the Lord. I love Jesus, and I'm going to stay with the Lord. All the prayers for me were not in vain."

Shortly afterwards, he came to visit Pam, bringing his Buddhist wife with him. Pam immediately took them to visit her spiritual mom, JoAnne. Before they left her house, JoAnne had led O'Brien's wife to Jesus.[12]

Tohuw people—lost, confused, deceived, spiritually barren—can be brought to salvation if the Holy Spirit is released to hover. Buddhists and rebellious brothers are not a problem for Him; that is, if we pray. Don't call them unsaved, call them pre-saved and get on with it.

The second example of the Holy Spirit hovering, bringing forth life out of lifelessness, is in Deuteronomy 32:10-18. All four of the previously mentioned Hebrew words are used in this passage: *tohuw, rachaph, yalad* and *chuwl*. In this passage Moses is recounting to the Israelites their history and speaks of Israel as an individual, obviously referring back to Abraham, the father of the nation. In verse 10, Moses says God found him in a *tohuw* situation—in other words, lifeless or barren.

Abraham was in the same barren condition the earth was in prior to the Creation. Neither he nor Sarah had the ability at this point to produce life. They were sterile, lifeless. We are then told in verse 11 that like an eagle hovers (*rachaphs*) over its young, the Lord hovered over them. The Holy Spirit brooded over Abraham and Sarah, releasing His life and power, giving them the ability to conceive!

We read in Hebrews 11:11 that by faith Sarah received *dunamis* (the miraculous power of the Holy Spirit)[13] to conceive. As He hovered, God was actually birthing a nation in them. Later in the passage (Deut. 32:18) *yalad* and *chuwl*, the primary Hebrew words for travail or giving birth, are used: "You neglected the Rock who begot you, and forgot the God who gave you birth." The identical words are chosen in this passage to describe the Holy Spirit's hovering over Abraham and Sarah to bring forth life as were used in the Genesis Creation and in Isaiah 66:8. The hovering that brought forth natural Israel will also bring forth spiritual Israel as He *rachaphs* through our intercession.

Our third example of the Holy Spirit bringing forth life as He hovered, or brooded over, is found in Luke 1:35, the conception of Christ in Mary. The angel of the Lord came to Mary telling her that she would bear a child. She responded by asking, "How can this be, since I am a virgin?" (v. 34).

The answer was, "The Holy Spirit will come upon you, and the power of the Most High will overshadow you" (v. 35). Overshadow is the Greek word *episkiazo*, which means "to cast a shade upon; to envelope in a haze of brilliancy; to invest with supernatural influence."[14] It is in some ways a counterpart for the Hebrew word *rachaph*. Thayer says it is used "of the Holy Spirit exerting creative energy upon the womb of the Virgin Mary and impregnating it."[15]

The word is only used three times in the New Testament. At the transfiguration of Jesus in Matthew 17:5, the passage says the cloud of the Lord "overshadowed" them. It is also used in Acts 5:15 when people were trying to get close to Peter—in his "shadow"—that they might be healed. Have you ever wondered how Peter's shadow could heal anyone? It didn't. What was actually happening was that the Holy Spirit was moving out from Peter—hovering and *rachaphing*—and when individuals stepped into the cloud, or overshadowing, they were healed.

God desperately wants to release His creative birthing powers through us to bring forth the fruit of Calvary.

Intercession releases the Holy Spirit to hover around an individual, enveloping that person with His power and life, bringing conviction of sin and breaking strongholds. We are His birthing vessels, His incubation chambers. He desperately wants to release His creative birthing power through us, bringing forth the fruit of Calvary. He wants to use us in *tohuw* (lifeless, fruitless, desolate, barren) situations, releasing His life into them. As He did at Creation, He wants to bring forth new creations in Christ Jesus.

As with Israel when He hovered over the barren bodies of Abraham and Sarah, bringing forth a nation, He wants to bring forth spiritual Israel from us. As with Mary when He hovered, bringing forth, or conceiving, the Christ in her, He desires to bring forth Christ in people through our intercession. Here's an excellent example:

One morning a phone call from her son interrupted Quin Sherrer's busy schedule. "Mom, my roommate's mother is dying of throat cancer in a military hospital near you," he said. "He has recently accepted Jesus, but he's concerned because his mother doesn't know the Lord. Would you go see her and pray for her?"

When Quin and her prayer partner, Fran, walked into the hospital room, Beatrice was in such pain she could barely talk. "Did you know your son Mickey has become a Christian?" Quin asked, getting right to the point of the visit. "My son rooms with him and has seen such a happy change in him. In fact, Mickey is concerned about your spiritual condition."

"Yes, he told me. I'm glad for him, but it's just too late for me," Beatrice said. Assuring her that it was not too late and that Jesus would accept her right where she was, Fran read several Scripture verses while Quin silently prayed that the Holy Spirit would come and hover around Beatrice, bringing forth new life.

Finally, Beatrice said that she was ready to ask Him to forgive her and be her Savior and Lord. She quietly prayed, "Lord Jesus, please forgive me for my rebellion and for running from You. Come live in my heart. I want to be Yours."

Quin visited her a few more times in the hospital, taking her a Bible and praying with her, before Beatrice died a few weeks later. While at the funeral home, Quin shared with Mickey regarding his mother's salvation experience. An elderly woman standing nearby spoke up, "Forgive me for listening in, but I'm Beatrice's mother. I can't remember a day when I didn't pray for my only daughter to come to the Lord."

"Well, dear, your prayers were answered," Quin said.

"She made it to heaven!" the woman exclaimed, wiping tears from her eyes. "She actually accepted Jesus just days before she died! Thank You, Jesus! Thank You, Lord, for Your faithfulness."[16]

The prayers of Beatrice's mother and son, as well as those of Quin and Fran, had released the creative, birthing power of the Holy Spirit to hover around Beatrice, bringing her to salvation.

Birthing Midwives—God's Word and Declarations of Faith

Decreeing God's Word and speaking forth Spirit-led declarations are two of the ways we release the birthing power of the Holy Spirit. They do not release Him in the sense that He is bound—God obviously is not bound. But, His creative power, energy and ability that come forth through His Word are released upon the earth as we speak them for Him. We are His partners, His representatives.

There is incredible power and creative ability in God's spoken Word. The Hebrew word *asah* is often used in association with the declared Word of God. *Asah* means "to work, do, make, create, construct, build and accomplish."[17] Nations, seas, the heavens and all creation are spoken of as being created (*asah*) by the word of God (see Pss. 33:6; 86:9; 95:5; 96:5; 148:1-6).

Listen to these other well-known verses that speak of God's Word accomplishing or creating:

God is not a man, that He should lie, nor a son of man, that He should repent. Has He said, and will He not do (*asah*) it? Or has He spoken, and will He not make it good? (Num. 23:19).

So shall My word be which goes forth from My mouth; it shall not return to Me empty, without accomplishing (*asah*) what I desire, and without succeeding in the matter for which I sent it (Isa. 55:11).

Then the LORD said to me, 'You have seen well, for I am watching over My word to perform (*asah*) it' (Jer. 1:12).

Please realize that when God said these things, He was not talking about speaking from the clouds. He was referring to what He had been saying and was still saying to people through His servants. In essence He was declaring. "These men's words are My words. They are My voice. Their words won't return to Me void, but will do exactly what I send them to do through these vessels. They will do, accomplish and perform—they will *asah*!"

We must understand that it is not an issue of what our words would normally do. It is rather speaking *for God* that releases His power to accomplish something. Isn't this what happens as we preach or declare the gospel, which "is the power of God for salvation" (Rom. 1:16)? Our mouths, speaking God's Word, release the power inherent in the gospel. This is also what happens when we speak His Word as a sword in spiritual warfare (see Eph. 6:17). He infuses our words with divine power. Holy Spirit-inspired declarations are powerful because they release the power of God into situations. We become the voice of God upon the earth.

Evelyn's Bible was marked with pen and tears as, for years, she prayed God's Word for her family. "I remember calling out Isaiah 49:25 and 54:13," she said, "reminding God that He would save our sons and daughter and that they would be taught of the Lord."

After visiting her son Ken on the East Coast, her heart was deeply grieved for him. On her return flight home, she prayed, "God, I know all the Scriptures that are there to stand on for my family, but I need something new and fresh so I can fight the good fight for my son." She opened a small book of Proverbs she had with her, and suddenly a verse seemed to leap off the page, birthing faith in her for Ken: "You can also be very sure that God will rescue the children of the godly" (Prov. 11:21, *TLB*). Wondering why she had never noticed this verse before, she realized this was a Bible version she usually didn't use. It was as though the Lord was saying to her, "You may know all the Scriptures, but you don't know all the versions!"

Little did Evelyn realize that ahead lay many years of prayer and warfare for Ken, as he became increasingly hard, bitter and angry. But Evelyn and her husband persevered in declaring the Word of God over their son, continuing to pray that God would indeed rescue him. Finally, the day came when Ken called to tell them he had repented and turned to the Lord.

"I'll never forget the moment he came home. There he stood, so visibly changed! Ken's countenance, dark for so many years, now was lit up with that inward glow that only Jesus can give."[18]

As this mother released the power of God over her son's life, the spoken Word of God accomplished what it was sent forth to do.

The word in the New Testament for "confession" is *homologia*, which means "say the same thing."[19] Biblical confession is saying what God says—no more, no less. If it isn't what God is saying about a situation, it does nothing. But if it is what He says, it accomplishes much.

The Word of God is called a "seed" in the Scriptures. The root word in Greek is *speiro*. *Spora* and *sperma* are variations of the word, both of which are translated "seed" in the New Testament. It is easy to see the English words "spore" and "sperm" in them.

God's method of reproducing or bringing forth life is His Word, by which we are born again (see 1 Pet. 1:23), cleansed (see John 15:3), matured (see Matt. 13:23), freed (see John 8:31,32), healed (see Ps. 107:20)—as well as many other results. When God speaks His Word, He is sprinkling seeds that will bring forth. The Word of God is never ineffective; it will always produce. When we speak God's Word into situations, as the Holy Spirit directs, we are sprinkling the seeds of God, which then gives Him the ability to cause life to come forth!

Job 22:28 declares, "You will also decree a thing, and it will be established for you." The word "decree" means literally "decide and decree"[20]—determines something and then decrees it. The actual meaning of *omer*, the word translated "thing" is "a word, a command, a promise."[21]

A more precise wording would be, "You shall decree or declare a word." Then He says it will be established for you. "Establish" is the word *qum*, meaning not only to establish but also to "arise or stand up."[22] Here's what I believe God is saying: "You shall decree a word and it will rise up. You shall sprinkle My seed. It will arise (grow) and establish something in the earth." Some would contend that we cannot command God to do something. I would agree. But there is a great difference between dictating and simply being a spokesperson. We are not telling God what to do. We are decreeing *for* Him, releasing His Word to perform its work.

Job 6:25 (*KJV*) reads: "How forcible are right words!" Forcible is the word *marats*, which also means "to press."[23] As the signet ring of a king presses a document with his seal, our words also seal things. They seal our salvation, the promises of God, our destinies and many other things (see Prov. 18:20-21; Matt. 12:37; Mark 11:23; Rom. 10:8-10).

Ecclesiastes 12:11 (*KJV*) tells us "The words of the wise are as goads, and as nails fastened by the masters of assemblies." Our words act as nails, constructing things in the spirit. Just as a nail is used to keep a board in place, words are used to keep God's promises in place, allowing them to build or construct (one of the meanings of *asah*) things in the spirit.

Ezekiel and the valley of dry bones is an example of declaration. "[Speak] to these bones!" (Ezek. 37:4, *AMP*), God said to the prophet.

Can you imagine what Ezekiel thought? *Speak to them? God, if You want something said to skeletons, why don't You just do it?* But Ezekiel obeyed and said, "O dry bones, hear the word of the Lord." And they did! Bone came to bone and flesh came on them.

There was no life in them, however, and Ezekiel's next assignment amazes me more than prophesying to the bones. The Lord told him *"Prophesy to the breath"* (v. 9). Later in the passage we're told that the breath he was prophesying to was the Holy Spirit. God didn't say, "Prophesy *by* the Holy Spirit," nor did He say, "Prophesy *for* the Holy Spirit." God said, "I want you to prophesy *to* the Holy Spirit." Ezekiel did and the Spirit of God did what a man told Him to. Incredible! Did the prophet actually command the Holy Spirit? Not really. He wasn't commanding God; He was commanding *for* God.

Apply these principles to intercession for the lost. As you declare God's Word over those for whom you pray, you are releasing the hovering of the Holy Spirit to birth the new creation (*asah*). Speak life and deliverance over them. Speak conviction, revelation and repentance. God will perform His Word.

QUESTIONS FOR WISDOM AND FAITH

1. What do you feel is the role of a Christian in God's birthing process?

2. Is it possible for us to negatively affect a spiritual birth in progress?

3. What is the critical element in spiritual birthing? Is it prayer, the Scriptures, declarations of faith . . . ?

4. When a new life in Christ is born, what are the critical nutrients for maturity and strength in Christ?

5. Should believers be experiencing numerous spiritual births in and around their lives each day?

Endnotes

Chapter 1

1. Quin Sherrer and Ruthanne Garlock, *How to Pray for Your Family and Friends* (Ann Arbor, MI: Servant Publications, 1990), p. 80.
2. Ibid., p. 81.

Chapter 2

1. James Strong, *The New Strong's Exhaustive Concordance of the Bible* (Nashville, TN: Thomas Nelson Publishers, 1990), Greek Dictionary, ref. no. 5287.
2. Ibid., ref. no. 1650.
3. Ibid., ref. no. 3358.
4. Ibid., ref. no. 5232.
5. Ibid., ref. no. 4135.
6. George Müller, *Release the Power of Prayer* (New Kensington, PA: Whitaker House, 1999), pp. 46, 47.
7. Alice Gray, *Stories for the Heart* (Sisters, OR: Multnomah Publishers, 1996), pp. 255-257.
8. Strong, *The New Strong's Exhaustive Concordance of the Bible*, Hebrew and Chaldee Dictionary, ref. no. 3467.
9. Charles G. Finney, *How to Experience Revival* (New Kensington, PA: Whitaker House, 1984), p. 58.
10. Craig Brian Larson, *Illustrations for Preaching and Teaching* (Grand Rapids, MI: Baker Books, 1993), p. 25.
11. Quin Sherrer and Ruthanne Garlock, *How to Pray for Your Family and Friends* (Ann Arbor, MI: Servant Publications, 1990), pp. 134, 135.

Chapter 3

1. Alice Gray, *Stories for the Heart* (Sisters, OR: Multnomah Publishers, 1996), p. 109.
2. Spiros Zodhiates, *The Complete Word Study Dictionary* (Iowa Falls, IA: Word Bible Publishers, 1992), p. 816.
3. James Strong, *The New Strong's Exhaustive Concordance of the Bible* (Nashville, TN: Thomas Nelson Publishers, 1990), Greek Dictionary, ref. no. 575.
4. W. E. Vine, *The Expanded Vine's Expository Dictionary of New Testament Words* (Minneapolis, MN: Bethany House Publishers, 1984), p. 125.

5. Strong, *The New Strong's Exhaustive Concordance of the Bible*, Greek Dictionary, ref. no. 5188.

6. Ibid., Greek Dictionary, ref. no. 5187.

7. Azriela Jaffe, *Heart Warmers* (Holbrook, MA: Adams Media Corporation, 2000), pp. 10-12.

8. Quin Sherrer and Ruthanne Garlock, *How to Pray for Your Family and Friends* (Ann Arbor, MI: Servant Publications, 1990), p. 44.

9. Strong, *The New Strong's Exhaustive Concordance of the Bible*, Greek Dictionary, ref. no. 1415.

10. Paul Billheimer, *Destined for the Throne* (Christian Literature Crusade: Fort Washington, PA, 1975), p. 67.

11. Zodhiates, *The Complete Word Study Dictionary*, p. 1464.

12. Ibid., p. 1463.

13. Edward K. Rowell, *Fresh Illustrations for Preaching and Teaching* (Grand Rapids, MI: Baker Books, 1997), p. 182.

14. Strong, *The New Strong's Exhaustive Concordance of the Bible*, Greek Dictionary, ref. no. 1124.

15. Ibid., Greek Dictionary, ref. no. 3056.

16. Spiros Zodhiates, *Hebrew-Greek Key Study Bible—New American Standard*, rev. ed. (Chattanooga, TN: AMG Publishers, 1990), p. 1718.

17. Ibid., p. 1858.

18. Ibid., p. 1834.

19. Ibid., p. 1856.

20. Robert J. Morgan, *Real Stories for the Soul* (Nashville, TN: Thomas Nelson Publishers, 2000), pp. 226, 227.

Chapter 4

1. James Strong, *The New Strong's Exhaustive Concordance of the Bible* (Nashville, TN: Thomas Nelson Publishers, 1990), Greek Dictionary, ref. no. 2192.

2. Ibid., ref. no. 2507.

3. Ibid., ref. no. 1415.

4. Quin Sherrer and Ruthanne Garlock, *How to Pray for Your Family and Friends* (Ann Arbor, MI: Servant Publications, 1990), pp. 158, 159.

5. Spiros Zodhiates, *The Complete Word Study Dictionary* (Iowa Falls, IA: Word Bible Publishers, 1992), p. 923.

6. Sherrer and Garlock, *How to Pray for Your Family and Friends*, pp. 163, 164.

7. Craig Brian Larson, *Illustrations for Preaching and Teaching* (Grand Rapids, MI: Baker Books, 1993), p. 239.

8. George Müller, *Release the Power of Prayer* (New Kensington, PA: Whitaker House, 1999), pp. 86, 87.
9. Edward K. Rowell, *Fresh Illustrations for Preaching and Teaching* (Grand Rapids, MI: Baker Books, 1997), p. 196.
10. Strong, *The New Strong's Exhaustive Concordance*, Greek Dictionary, ref. no. 5313.
11. Walter Bauer, *A Greek-English Lexicon of the New Testament* (Chicago: The University of Chicago Press, 1979), p. 386.
12. Sherrer and Garlock, *How to Pray for Your Family and Friends*, pp. 36, 37.
13. Zodhiates, *Hebrew-Greek Key Study Bible—New American Standard*, p. 1797.
14. Robert J. Morgan, *Real Stories for the Soul* (Nashville, TN: Thomas Nelson Publishers, 2000), pp. 141-143.

Chapter 5

1. Robert J. Morgan, *Real Stories for the Soul* (Nashville, TN: Thomas Nelson Publishers, 2000), pp. 199-201.
2. Charles G. Finney, *How to Experience Revival* (New Kensington, PA: Whitaker House, 1984), pp. 49, 50.
3. Ibid., p. 12.
4. Spiros Zodhiates, *Hebrew-Greek Key Study Bible—New American Standard* (Chattanooga, TN: AMG Publishers, 1990), p. 1723.
5. James Strong, *The New Strong's Exhaustive Concordance* (Nashville, TN: Thomas Nelson Publishers, 1990), Hebrew and Chaldee Dictionary, ref. no. 4997.
6. "More Than Her Car," *Parables, Etc.*, July 1995, http://www.autoillustrator.com (accessed February 1, 2000).

Chapter 6

1. Quin Sherrer and Ruthanne Garlock, *Praying Prodigals Home* (Ventura, CA: Regal Books, 2000), adapted from pp. 89, 90.
2. W. E. Vine, *The Expanded Vine's Expository Dictionary of New Testament Words* (Minneapolis, MN: Bethany House Publishers, 1984), p. 110.
3. James Strong, *The New Strong's Exhaustive Concordance of the Bible* (Nashville, TN: Thomas Nelson Publishers, 1990), Greek Dictionary, ref. no. 4057.
4. Ibid., ref. no. 5228.
5. Ibid., ref. no. 2596.
6. Joseph Henry Thayer, *A Greek-English Lexicon of the New Testament* (Grand Rapids, MI: Baker Book House, 1977), p. 422.

7. Sherrer and Garlock, *Praying Prodigals Home*, adapted from pp. 124, 125.

8. Strong, *The New Strong's Exhaustive Concordance of the Bible*, Hebrew and Chaldee Dictionary, ref. no. 8414.

9. Spiros Zodhiates, *Hebrew-Greek Key Study Bible—New American Standard*, rev. ed. (Chattanooga, TN: AMG Publishers, 1990), p. 1790.

10. C. F. Keil and F. Delitzsch, *Commentary on the Old Testament*, vol. 1 (Grand Rapids, MI: Williams B. Eerdmans, 1991), p. 48.

11. William Wilson, *Old Testament Word Studies* (Grand Rapids, MI: Kregel Publications, 1978), p. 175.

12. Sherrer and Garlock, *Praying Prodigals Home*, adapted from pp. 131-133.

13. Strong, *The New Strong's Exhaustive Concordance of the Bible*, Greek Dictionary, ref. no. 1411.

14. Ibid., ref. no. 1982.

15. Thayer, *A Greek-English Lexicon of the New Testament*, p. 242.

16. Quin Sherrer, *Good Night, Lord* (Ventura, CA: Regal Books, 2000), pp. 197, 198.

17. Zodhiates, *Hebrew-Greek Key Study Bible—New American Standard*, p. 1763.

18. Sherrer and Garlock, *Praying Prodigals Home*, adapted from pp. 47-49.

19. Zodhiates, *Hebrew-Greek Key Study Bible—New American Standard*, p. 1861.

20. R. Laird Harris, Gleason L. Archer Jr. and Bruce K. Waltke, *Theological Wordbook of the Old Testament* (Grand Rapids, MI: Williams B. Eerdmans, 1991), p, 158.

21. Ibid., p. 118.

22. Ibid., p. 793.

23. Strong, *The New Strong's Exhaustive Concordance of the Bible*, Hebrew and Chaldee Dictionary, ref. no. 4834.

REGAL BOOKS BY
DUTCH SHEETS

How to Pray for Lost Loved Ones

God's Timing for Your Life

Watchman Prayer

The River of God

Intercessory Prayer

*For information about other resources by
Dutch Sheets, call or write:*

*Dutch Sheets Ministries
1015 Garden of the Gods
Colorado Springs, CO 80907
Phone (719) 548-8226*

Or visit Dutch Sheets Ministries online at:

www.dutchsheets.org